HEAR THE REAL-LIFE CASE . . .
MAKE YOUR JUDGMENT!

A California woman surprised her husband one evening with the news that she wanted a divorce. The couple ended their marriage with the standard legal proceedings; unfortunately the man's ex-wife simply forgot to mention to the court that a few days prior to deciding on the divorce, she had won over a million dollars in the lottery.

A couple of years later, the ex-husband learned the truth when he inadvertently received a letter in the mail offering to turn the lottery winner's money into ready cash. He filed suit against his ex-wife, and the case went to court.

Did the ex-husband deserve a portion of his ex-wife's lottery winnings? If so, how much?

You Be the Judge . . .

OUTCOME #31

The judge ruled that the ex-husband deserved ALL of it, penalizing the woman for defrauding her ex-husband and the court. The woman proceeded to file for bankruptcy.

100 INCREDIBLE, PROVOCATIVE, AND FASCINATING REAL-LIFE CASES

COURT*TV*

YOU BE THE JUDGE

PATRICK J. SAUER

WARNER BOOKS

An AOL Time Warner Company

Cover design by Jerry Pfeifer

Warner Books, Inc.
1271 Avenue of the Americas
New York, NY 10020

Visit our Web site at
www.twbookmark.com.

 An AOL Time Warner Company

Printed in the United States of America

First Printing: April 2002

10 9 8 7 6 5 4 3 2 1

ACKNOWLEDGMENTS

I would like to thank Jessica Faust, Jackie Joiner, Bookends, John Talbot, Mom, Dad and Kim Kurowski. I am also indebted to the American legal system for all of its inherent triumphs and flaws, and for its members, who have explained how it works on a firsthand basis.

INTRODUCTION

Where were you on October 3, 1995 at 1 P.M. E.S.T.?

Can't recall? Seems way too long ago?

As they say on all the television courtroom dramas, let me "rephrase."

Where were you when you heard the words that stopped a country in its tracks . . . the words that declared Orenthal James Simpson "not guilty" on all counts?

Now do you remember where you were?

I know where I was—in a retail store of some kind across the street from Boston Common with two large television screens zeroed in on the Los Angeles courtroom that we had all lived in month after month after month. Before re-creating the moment of truth, let me back up a bit to the hour preceding the climax. I had a meeting with a dean at a potential graduate program scheduled for Tuesday at 12:30 P.M. and had been immersed in filling out applications and writing essays in the week before the end of the trial, so it had more or less dropped off my radar screen. I was never an O.J. trial junkie to begin with, more of a casual observer, so I couldn't for the life of me figure out why the dean was rushing through our discussion and abruptly ended the meeting before I had a chance to ask any questions. I walked outside to the empty streets of Beantown and headed down the block trying to figure out what had transpired when I saw a store packed with people staring at a television.

The verdict is in, chucklehead.

The verdict is in.

I entered the store moments before the famous (or infamous, depending on your P.O.V.) "not guilty" verdict was announced. One couldn't help but notice the varying degrees of responses: two African-American gentlemen high-fived, an angry man of Irish descent used words unfit for family programming, there were a few derisive jokes, a few stunned looks, and the response that seemed to sum it all up from an unimposing, diminutive elderly woman, "What the hell are we going to do now?"

Regardless of your feelings about the verdict in the O.J. trial (or its civil sequel), one point can't be denied—it was a conversation piece.

And, oh, what a conversation piece it was.

Legal, political, social, racial, sexual, psychological, physical, procedural, philosophical—pick a word that ends in "al" and it was wrapped up in the "Trial of the Century." It got people talking . . . and talking . . . and talking. Pundits were all over the television, but there were just as many in the coffee shop. I was working in a Philadelphia office, where a white woman told me, "look at him on the stand, does O.J. look like a murderer? No chance." To which her black coworker responded, "No question he's guilty, but I bet he walks." The trial was on everyone's lips, and everyone had an opinion they wanted to share. For good and bad, it became a national debate on topics as varied as domestic abuse, racist cops, the nature of celebrity, and how fast Ben & Jerry's ice cream melts.

USA Today reported at the time that a study commissioned by the Cambridge Human Resource Group estimated that the country lost $40 billion in workplace time throughout the trial. *Forty billion dollars* in e-mails, phone calls, break-room diatribes and watercooler digressions. The mother ship of this very book, *Court TV*, saw its ratings increase 1,000 percent. And when the verdict was read, everyone from President Clinton on down was glued to the screen. Roughly 108 million people, 57 percent of American adults, listened to the words "not guilty" right along with O.J. Simpson. The United States of America came to a standstill, in the middle of the work week, long distance calls were down over 50 percent from 1-1:20 P.M. according to AT&T.

The "Trial of the Century" was the conversation of the year, and the year before that, and the year before that, and the year before that . . . and it still lingers today. If nothing else, the O.J. saga got people gabbing and it is in the spirit of deliberation that *You Be the Judge* was written.

You Be the Judge is a collection of wild, offbeat, perplexing, intriguing, maddening court cases for you and your dinner guests to discuss civilly or parley loudly, depending on powers of persuasion. The cases in the book have been altered a bit—most names, dates, and some locales have been removed— because it is intended to be used solely for amateurs. Professionals can continue using those thick books they always refer to on *Law & Order*. So, gather a group of friends (or enemies if you want to make it interesting), uncork a bottle of wine, and delve into these legal conundrums. Remember, there is only one instruction from the bench . . .

You Be the Judge.

COURT*TV*

You
BE THE
JUDGE

ENTRY #1

In a hotel parking lot, two men from out of town are shot in what police suspect was a drug deal gone sour. The two men, however, see it differently and sue the hotel for failing to provide ample security, which could have prevented the shooting. A lawsuit is brought against the hotel on the grounds that the hotel chain was negligent in protecting its parking lot.

Should a hotel be held liable for a shooting in its parking lot? Even if it is lacking in security measures?

You be the judge . . .

OUTCOME #1

The jury awarded the two men $1.7 million, after the trial judge banned any evidence that the men may have been involved in a drug deal on the grounds that it could have unfairly influenced the outcome.

ENTRY #2

A freelance reporter for National Public Radio was doing an investigative piece on child pornography. He initially went into chat rooms to talk to those who get their kicks from illegal sexual images of children, but whenever he came clean and announced he was a reporter, the conversations would stop cold. The reporter decided to gain the trust of his subjects by keeping his identity secret and by sending out roughly 160 pictures to his on-line interviewees (a common ploy used by criminals to prevent police infiltration).

The reporter was charged with multiple felony counts of sending and receiving child pornography over the Internet. Federal prosecutors contend that the reporter's intent was not journalistic and that he simply wanted his own collection of illegal pictures. NPR went on record as saying the story was never assigned, but the reporter insisted he was working on a story. A U.S. District Court judge ruled that the reporter could not mount a First Amendment defense, because child pornography is not protected by the right to free speech.

Is it ever all right for a journalist to break the law? Can the reporter's intent ever be known? How can a story be written about the underground cyberworld of child pornography if the source can't be investigated?

You be the judge . . .

OUTCOME #2

The reporter copped a plea and pleaded guilty to one count of transmitting and one count of receiving child pornography. The ruling against mounting a First Amendment case was appealed, but to no avail.

ENTRY #3

A police officer in Pennsylvania entered a bar with an arrest warrant for a man we'll call Myron. After arresting Myron and taking him outside, the cop learned that Bob had sold drugs to Myron's brother moments before in the bar. He went back inside and asked Bob if he could pat him down, which produced a wad of cash and crack cocaine.

Bob was arrested and charged with possession of drugs with the intent to deliver. The police officer never mentioned to Bob that he had the right to refuse the search without a warrant. Bob's lawyer argued that since his client was not informed of his right to refuse a warrantless search, it was invalid and the case had to be thrown out of court.

Should the police be required to inform suspects of their right to refuse a search without a warrant? Should Bob face the music or get a free pass?

You be the judge . . .

OUTCOME #3

The Pennsylvania Superior (and Supreme) Court upheld the initial ruling (and federal standard) that as long as the police officer got the suspect's voluntary consent, the search was valid and permissible. Had Bob refused, or simply kept his mouth shut, the search would have been "unreasonable" under the Fourth Amendment to the Constitution.

ENTRY #4

The Internet has introduced all sorts of new legal conundrums, for instance, this case from Washington state. In a chat room, a man made contact with a police detective who was undercover as a young adolescent girl. The sting was set up after the police department was tipped off that the man had been sending child pornography out on the Internet and was making plans to meet teenage girls. The police officer crafted a phony cyberidentity and built a relationship with the man who ultimately propositioned the fictional girl for sexual intercourse. After dining with his wife, the man went to meet the girl and instead found the police officer, who arrested him and charged him with second-degree attempted rape.

The case in question is intriguing because Washington's Privacy Act mandates consent of both parties before conversations made over "any electronic device" can be recorded. Police frequently seek court orders to wiretap a person's phone line, which they did not do in this sting operation. The man's lawyers argued that the on-line relationship in the chat room constituted a private conversation and the transcripts should not be allowed as evidence.

Should the computer conversations be considered private? Are they different than telephone calls? Should they be allowed as evidence?

You be the judge . . .

OUTCOME #4

A Washington judge ruled that the police did not violate the Privacy Act and chat rooms do not have the same protections as telephone calls. Court permission to record and transcribe the cyberdiscourse isn't necessary because the computer, unlike the telephone, is a recording device unto itself, which is common knowledge. The transcripts were allowed and the man was convicted and sentenced to seven and a half years in prison.

ENTRY #5

The First Amendment has led to some of the most polarizing and complex legal cases in American history and the stakes are constantly and consistently raised. A recent doozy is a radical right-to-life group's Abortionists on Trial website. The site lists abortion doctors across the United States and equates them with the Nuremberg defendants and calls them "baby butchers." The website also includes personal information on many of the doctors, all of which is perfectly legal.

The site entered a different realm when the names of every abortion doctor who has been killed were crossed out. After Dr. Barnett Slepian was murdered in his home in front of his children, a line reportedly marked him off the list almost instantaneously. A consortium of doctors, Planned Parenthood, and women's clinic employees sued the website under a federal law that prohibits violence and threats against abortion doctors.

Should the Abortionists on Trial website be protected

under the First Amendment? If it doesn't technically encourage violence, harassment, or murder of abortion doctors and clinic employees, should the speech be allowed? Who should decide what can and can't be said, no matter how offensive it may be to you personally? If the website is banned, is the radical prolife group that started the list a victim of censorship? Are its opinions, ideas, and topics being suppressed?

On the other hand, is the group hiding behind the First Amendment while putting doctors and their families (children and home addresses are included) in grave danger? Isn't this a provocation to kill in the name of God and the radicals' version of morality?

You be the judge . . .

OUTCOME #5

A federal jury ruled against the Abortionists on Trial website as a violation of the statute against the harassment of abortion doctors. A federal judge later issued a restraining order against updates on the list or copycats of any sort of the Wanted posters. The owner of the site vowed to keep it on the Internet and added that he intended to put up live camera feeds from various abortion clinics.

There are free-speech advocates who feel this is a violation of the First Amendment and see a slippery slope to a ban on all kinds of inflammatory speech. It is a case that won't be going away anytime soon and will constantly be reinvented in one form or another because of the deceptively simple question . . .

What constitutes free speech?

ENTRY #6

Freedom of religion is one of the fundamental tenents of free societies around the globe, but this unimaginable case from Britain tested the extreme limits of the rights of personal religious beliefs over family welfare. Siamese twins joined at the abdomen were born to a deeply devout Roman Catholic family that had traveled from a poor, remote area in Eastern Europe for advanced treatment. Sadly, only one baby had lungs and the twins shared a damaged heart which was struggling to supply oxygen to the babies and their condition was rapidly worsening. Doctors gave them a maximum of six months to live unless they were separated. The family said in a statement to the court that killing one to save the other was not God's will, as everyone has the right to life.

Should the family have the right to follow its religious beliefs, or is the welfare of the baby the most important priority? Keep in mind that there is no chance that the baby without lungs or functioning heart can live after separation.

There is a great risk both will die simultaneously if they continue to share the damaged heart, in which case no successful operation to separate the twin with a lung after the other died would be possible.

You be the judge . . .

OUTCOME #6

In a case so complex that King Solomon himself might have thrown up his hands in despair, the English judges ruled that the baby who was effectively providing life-support for her sister must be saved. In an amazing wrinkle, a Roman Catholic Italian cardinal offered a "safe haven" at a hospital in his country, where the family wouldn't have to separate them. The legal possibility arose of whether the Siamese twins would become wards of the state, thus preventing them from traveling to Italy without the court's permission, regardless of the desire of the parents. The babies were separated in an operation in England and one survived as expected.

ENTRY #7

The rights of law enforcement versus the rights of American citizens is always a subject worthy of legal wrangling. Here is a simple scenario that divided state courts across the country and eventually made it all the way to the top—the Supreme Court.

A man or woman stands on the corner minding his or her own business, not participating in any sort of illegal activity. A police officer comes walking toward said person and he or she takes off. There was no prior suspicious behavior, so does running away constitute legal grounds for a chase by the police officer? Is evidence obtained after the person is caught usable? Why would any innocent person hightail it from the fuzz? Is the hundred meter dash probable cause in and of itself?

You be the judge (or in this case, the Justice) . . .

OUTCOME #7

In a 5–4 decision, the Supreme Court ruled that running away from a police officer is a legitimate reason for the cop to give chase. Chief Justice William Rehnquist said "Allowing officers confronted with such flight to stop the fugitive and investigate further is quite consistent with the individual's right to go about his business or to stay put and remain silent in the face of police questioning . . . Headlong flight—wherever it occurs—is the consummate act of evasion."

Just something to keep in mind the next time you feel like testing your wheels in the face of Johnny Law.

ENTRY #8

Here's an important case in the history of the modern civil rights era that will show how much things have changed, but will also require that your mind-set be filtered through the "Wayback" machine into Virginia in 1960.

An African-American law student at Howard University was riding on a Trailways bus from Washington to Alabama. During a layover in Virginia, the student entered a segregated diner, sat down in the white section, and ordered a bite to eat. Asked to move into the colored section, the student refused saying that he was protected by *federal* anti-segregation laws because he was an *interstate* passenger. He was promptly arrested, charged with trespassing, and fined.

The Commonwealth of Virginia conceded that the student's conviction would have to be dismissed if anything in the Constitution or federal law gave him the right to sit and be served in the restaurant wherever he pleased. The Commonwealth of Virginia stated that it found no such right, so

NAACP lawyers petitioned the Supreme Court and Thurgood Marshall pleaded their case before the justices he would soon join.

At question was the nature of the relationship between the privately contracted restaurant and the Trailways terminal. The Bus Terminal Restaurant of Richmond, Inc., provided meals for Trailways passengers, but the only interest the bus company had was the annual rent and a small share of the gross profits. If the restaurant didn't fall under the Interstate Commerce Act, which outlawed "unjust discrimination," then it was not beholden to federal law and could run its business any way it saw fit.

Set aside the immorality and illegality of segregation for a moment and ask yourself, did the restaurant have the legal right to segregate its customers and should the arrest and fine stand? Or, in simpler, broader terms, should the federal government have been able to tell a small business how to run its eatery? If so, what argument would you have presented to help wipe the Howard law student's slate clean?

You be the judge . . .

OUTCOME #8

This case turned out to be extremely important in the annals of civil rights legislation. In a 7–2 decision, the Supreme Court ruled in favor of the student, in no small part because the manager of the restaurant said that the clientele was mainly Trailways passengers. Justice Hugo L. Black wrote, "Interstate passengers have to eat, and they have a right to expect that this essential transportation food service . . . would be rendered without discrimination prohibited by the Interstate Commerce Act."

A partnership was formed between the federal judiciary and the civil rights movement, and this was one of the first blows that helped tear down the walls of segregation. It is hard to believe that the dismantling of segregation would need the guiding light of the Interstate Commerce Act, but it had strong repercussions and in August 1960, the Bus Terminal Restaurants, Inc., of Raleigh, North Carolina declared that racial segregation would no longer be permitted in its establishments.

ENTRY #9

War often brings out the best in America, uniting the citizenry for a common goal, which by its very nature needs a common enemy. But what if the "enemy" is an American who may have been simply in the wrong place at the wrong time? The infamous "Tokyo Rose" trial took place in San Francisco when Iva Toguri was the accused in one of only seven American treason trials following World War II.

Toguri was born in Los Angeles and raised an American by parents who had emigrated from Japan. In the summer of 1941 she paid a visit to a sickly aunt in her ancestral home and stayed with relatives while she attended to her aunt. After the bombing of Pearl Harbor on December 7, 1941, Toguri was stuck in Japan, and her primary marketable skill was her knowledge of English. After typing for a variety of news outlets, Toguri was forced to become one of the female announcers for Radio Tokyo, collectively called "Tokyo Rose" by American soldiers. Toguri mostly played popular music and delivered the occasional pro-Japanese propaganda statement written by her supervisors.

There were roughly ten thousand Japanese-Americans in Japan during World War II, but only a few were arrested. Toguri, who had called herself the "one and only Tokyo Rose" after a lucrative offer from two American journalists, was one of them. She was picked up in Tokyo and brought to California to stand trial for treason.

Keeping in mind that there have been American soldiers who refused to cooperate with the enemy, even at great personal risk, was Toguri guilty of treason? Even if she had been forced to participate?

You be the judge . . .

OUTCOME #9

The trial of "Tokyo Rose" was contentious to say the least. Toguri pleaded innocent to the eight charges of treason leveled against her. After a three-month trial the all-white jury was deadlocked, but the judge ordered them to deliberate until they reached a verdict.

Eventually, the nine jurors who found Toguri guilty convinced the three remaining holdouts and she was sentenced to ten years in prison and a ten-thousand-dollar fine. After six years Toguri was released for good behavior, but whether she received a fair trial was always in question. In 1977, as his last act as president, Gerald Ford pardoned Toguri, and the citizenship of "Tokyo Rose" was fully restored.

ENTRY #10

Here's a surefire case that always sparks up a good debate and fuels the flames of what our national symbols represent and how they should be treated.

In 1984, a staunch supporter of the American communist movement doused an American flag in kerosene and lit it at a protest outside the Republican National Convention in Dallas, Texas. Nobody was injured and the only property destroyed was the flag itself. Police arrested the protester and he was charged under a Texas law that made it illegal to "intentionally or knowingly desecrate . . . a state or national flag." The protester was convicted and sentenced to a year in prison and a $2,000 fine, a decision upheld by the Court of Appeals of Dallas, but overturned by the Texas Court of Criminal Appeals on the grounds that it violated the First Amendment. The case was appealed to the United States Supreme Court and argued in 1989.

Simple enough, is desecrating the American flag a crime? You be the judge . . .

OUTCOME #10

Whether it turns your stomach or not, the Supreme Court upheld the decision 6–3, making flag-burning a legal form of political protest. The decision stated, "We do not consecrate the flag by punishing its desecration, for in doing so we dilute the freedom that this cherished emblem represents."

ENTRY #11

And while we are on the subject of freedom of expression, here's a civil liberties doozy from the Heartland. A seventh-grade Kansas student drew a Confederate flag during math class and was suspended for violating the school's "zero-tolerance" policy. The racial harassment policy was a district wide policy that was read aloud by teachers, who were then asked to sign it. The policy was the result of a large task force of community members concerned about "racial tension." The demographics of the school had changed, and there had been an increase in racially-motivated fights, slurs, graffiti, and messages on T-shirts. To combat this, the district policy in question forbids students from wearing or possessing material that is "racially divisive or creates ill will or hatred."

The task force was encouraged to make the punishment for violating the guidelines severe and the Confederate flag was considered offensive and banned. An attorney on behalf of the student argued that the suspension violated his rights under the First Amendment. Records showed that the student had been suspended from school for one day in a previous year for making a racial comment in which the student allegedly used another derogatory term for African-Americans. At that time, the assistant principal chose to review the school's racial harassment policy with the teen instead of ordering a suspension.

Does the student have the right to draw a Confederate flag if he or she so chooses or was the suspension warranted? If the "Stars 'N Bars" is offensive, what about an African-American student sporting a Louis Farrakhan T-shirt? What about an Arab-American student with an anti-Israel poster in his locker? How about a student of any color who wears a political button supporting a ballot initiative that strictly limits immigration?

Should the suspension stand, or is the student's sketch of a Confederate flag a right protected by the Constitution?

You be the judge . . .

OUTCOME #11

The student was suspended for three days, and, two years later, a federal appeals court panel upheld the punishment. The panel ruled that the student knew the drawing was a violation of the "zero-tolerance" policy, even if he or she did not intentionally mean to harass a fellow student. The appeals panel said, "Given the school's need to be able to impose disciplinary sanctions for a wide range of unanticipated conduct disruptive of the educational process . . . school disciplinary rules need not be as detailed as a criminal code which imposes criminal sanctions." The student's appeal on the grounds that his right to free speech had been violated was turned away by the U.S. Supreme Court.

Here's another question to ponder: While the drawing of a Confederate flag violates a Kansas school policy, should a single school policy supersede the First Amendment of the Constitution?

ENTRY #12

A disabled man sued Wal-Mart after he was forced to park in a regular parking space because employees had used the handicapped parking spots during an outdoor sale. The man was angry enough at the low-price behemoth to ask for $5,000 in Small Claims Court.

Should the retail giant pay for blocking the handicapped parking space?

You be the judge . . .

OUTCOME #12

The court found in favor of the plaintiff and awarded him $1 in damages; Wal-Mart appealed the decision on the grounds that they had done nothing wrong, lost again, and the case ended up costing them $1,000 in court costs and damages to the plaintiff.

ENTRY #13

You think Leo DiCaprio and Kate Winslet had it rough on the *Titanic*? Check out this fascinating case from the maritime archives.

In 1841, an American ship, the *William Brown*, left England for Philadelphia with a load of cargo, 65 passengers and seventeen crewmen. Two hundred fifty miles off the coast of Newfoundland, the *William Brown* rammed into an iceberg and began a rapid descent into the icy waters of the Atlantic. There were two lifeboats—the captain and most of the crew took the small boat and the passengers climbed aboard the larger boat with First Mate Francis Rhodes and seaman Alexander Holmes (all except for the thirty-one passengers who went down with the *William Brown* because there wasn't enough space). The boats stayed together through the night, but the captain decided there was a better chance of being rescued if they split up. Rhodes told the captain that his boat was overcrowded and that they would have to lighten the load in order not to capsize.

Conditions worsened, and the boat was taking on too much water from the rain and the waves. Rhodes decided that their only chance of survival was to throw some passengers overboard. Holmes and the other crewmen threw fourteen single men into the freezing water and two women who were sisters to one of the men and wanted to die with their kin. The next day, the lifeboat was spotted and the survivors were rescued. The saga of the *William Brown* spread throughout Philadelphia and caused a fair amount of public outrage. The U.S. Attorney charged Rhodes and Holmes with manslaughter, which is a lesser charge than murder because it is defined as killing without malice. Rhodes disappeared, so Holmes stood trial alone.

Holmes's lawyers argued that it was an act of self-preservation and that he didn't have to wait until the absolute last possible moment because then the boat would have sunk and they all would have drowned. The judge instructed the jury that there are exceptions to self-preservation, one of which is when a person accepts the responsibility that implies putting his life at risk before taking the lives of others, a duty accepted by seaman.

Should Alexander Holmes have faced criminal charges in the deaths of the sixteen passengers he threw into the Atlantic Ocean?

You be the judge . . .

OUTCOME #13

The jury deliberated for sixteen hours before they reluctantly found Holmes guilty, accompanying the verdict with a plea for mercy. Holmes was sentenced to six months in prison and fined $20. The case established that self-preservation was not always a justifiable defense if the accused was, in effect, the caretaker of the deceased.

ENTRY #14

A Florida man who was convicted of killing his first wife twelve years prior, filed for custody of the daughter he had with his second wife. They divorced after nine years of marriage. Three years later—now on his third marriage—the father claimed that he could give the eleven-year-old girl a better environment than the girl's biological mother.

Why did the man believe that he should have custody of his daughter? Because her mother is now a lesbian. The attorney for the father said that the daughter "should have the opportunity to live in what we would refer to as a traditional family setting with traditional family values." The attorney said that his client had been rehabilitated since he fatally shot his first wife. He had served eight years in prison for second-degree murder and was fit to raise the child.

Who should get custody of their daughter, gay mom or killer dad?

You be the judge . . .

OUTCOME #14

The initial ruling by the circuit judge granted custody of the daughter to the child's father, citing the mother's sexual orientation and noting that the child "should be given the opportunity and the option to live in a non-lesbian world." The girl's mother received standard visiting privileges, but she appealed the decision on the grounds that Florida law clearly states that evidence must show a child has been harmed to change a custody order. The appeals court agreed with the trial judge, and primary custody went to the father.

ENTRY #15

While a soldier was out carousing, he met a young woman and took her for drinks and dancing. During one of the numbers, the woman collapsed into his arms, an event which he saw as a golden opportunity.

Assuming his date was passed out, the soldier took the woman to his car and had sexual "relations" with her. The problem was that the woman hadn't passed out.

She was dead.

Is the soldier guilty of a crime? And, if so, what would you charge him with?

You be the judge . . .

OUTCOME #15

Necrophilia charges were never filed, but the solider was tried and convicted of . . . attempted rape.

ENTRY #16

A 35-year-old Israeli man who had been sentenced to ten years for violent offenses (and had already spent the better part of twenty-one years behind bars), had a simple request. The prisoner repeatedly made it known that he wanted an inflatable woman to call his own.

The man sued the Prison Service over his right to share his cell with an inflatable sex doll.

Does the lonely prisoner have the right to a latex companion to live out his days in lockup? Are there other reasons beyond the simple fact that he's a prisoner?

You be the judge . . .

OUTCOME #16

The Supreme Court of Israel sided with the prison authorities and denied the man a plastic playmate. The reasons, however, were more than what might be expected. The Supreme Court felt the man could use the doll to fool wardens in an escape attempt (see *Escape from Alcatraz* with Clint Eastwood), hide or smuggle drugs into the prison, or the lovely lass could lead to brawls among the jealous inmates.

The prisoner did state that he would drop his request for a doll if the prison authorities would simply allow him to be with a woman. The request was denied.

But certainly a noble sacrifice, wouldn't you agree?

ENTRY #17

There once was an Orange County serial killer on death row who claimed that he was innocent of all sixteen murders. Since he believed he was innocent, he firmly objected to being characterized as a serial killer. He felt the label was false and deceptive and besmirched his good name.

An author wrote a book about the convicted serial killer, who felt that it was a work of fiction which would cause him to be rejected by society and keep him from securing gainful employment once he was let back into private life. The convicted killer sued the author for over $60 million, even though he had been convicted and was awaiting execution.

Does the serial killer's lawsuit have any merit?

You be the judge . . .

OUTCOME #17

The answer plain and simple: NO CHANCE. The lawsuit was thrown out in forty-six seconds.

The verdict was appealed and turned down by The California Supreme Court, but it still cost the writer's publisher some $30,000 in legal fees.

ENTRY #18

Is it a crime not to belong to a certain ethnic group? Let's take a look . . .

A member of a Native American church was indicted for importing peyote through the mail with the intent to distribute. He had shipped a quantity of peyote from Mexico to his home in New Mexico. He was going to use it in bona fide religious ceremonies of the Native American church to which he belonged. It is legal under the First Amendment for Native Americans to freely exercise their religion through the ceremonial use of peyote, though the federal government classifies it as an illegal hallucinogen.

The problem was that the man was not a Native American.

The United States brought the case against the man and argued that the protection applies only to members of the church who are American Indians. The United States claimed that the definition is people whose "ethnic descent is at least twenty-five percent derived from American Indian stock, and to the spouses of such persons," neither of which applied to the man in question.

So, who is in the right here: the man whose religious services utilize the psychedelic cactus? Or, the federal government and its assertion that the man imported illegal drugs and didn't qualify for a religious exemption?

You be the judge . . .

OUTCOME #18

The New Mexico judge who heard the case agreed with the man's motion to dismiss because the case violated his First Amendment right to freedom of religion. The judge felt it violated the Constitution to racially restrict who qualified as members of a certain church, in this case a non-Native American. He also noted that the "war on drugs" was eroding the guarantees in the Fourth and Fifth Amendments to the Constitution.

ENTRY #19

In 1984, at a Massachusetts county jail, prisoners sued for being subject to cruel and unusual living conditions in institutions constructed before the Civil War. The examples of said conditions included: cells without sinks or toilets (they had to use buckets), overcrowding with three or four inmates to a cell, and a lack of a winter exercise facility.

Does this sound like cruel and unusual living conditions? You be the judge . . .

OUTCOME #19

In an outcome that is sure to rile many of you, the inmates were awarded $2 million out of the pockets of Massachusetts taxpayers. Each prisoner who was part of the lawsuit received a tax-free payment of $10 for each day served in jail. The award not only included damages, but 12 percent interest was tacked on from the time the case was finally settled in 1991 until they collected their cash.

ENTRY #20

In 1868, a poor woman named Hester Vaughan stood trial for the murder of her newborn baby. Vaughan had traveled from England to America to be with her fiancé, who had another family and left her high and dry. Vaughan took a housekeeping job in Philadelphia, where she was raped by a household member and became pregnant.

She left her job and began renting a tiny room, barely making ends meet as a seamstress. Details are sketchy, but what is known is that, in early February 1868, Vaughan gave birth. She was malnourished, and her room had no heat in the heart of winter. Two days later, she asked another person living in the house for a box in which to place a dead infant and to please keep the matter secret.

The police were called, and Vaughan was arrested on murder charges. The *Philadelphia Inquirer* covered the case, and Vaughan claimed she accidentally fell on the child after being startled by a woman delivering coffee. A doctor from the coroner's office found several fractures of the skull and clots of blood between the brain and skull. The coffee lady testified that she heard one or two faint cries from the infant. Vaughan's lawyer, whom she hadn't seen from the time he took her payment until the first day of the trial, argued that she might have been bereft of reason and that the infant's death could have been an accident, and nobody could say different because she was the only witness.

An all-male jury found Vaughan guilty and a male judge sentenced her to die. A female doctor visited Vaughan in prison and after numerous interviews and a thorough medical examination determined that she was delirious with sickness and nearly frozen when she went into labor and most likely injured the child while trying to assist herself. The doctor questioned whether the infant was even born alive, contradicting court testimony, and wrote Governor Geary asking for a pardon. When Geary ignored the request, Vaughan's case was adopted by women's rights leaders like Susan B. Anthony and Elizabeth Cady Stanton who sent a resolution to Geary and some major newspapers arguing for Vaughan's pardon.

Did Vaughan deserve a pardon? And, if so, upon what grounds?

You be the judge . . .

OUTCOME #20

The resolution sent out by women's rights groups said that Vaughan did not receive a trial by a jury of her peers because women weren't allowed to vote or sit on a jury in 1868. It noted that women had no say in electing the judge who pronounced her sentence or the sheriff who might perform her execution.

The women's rights groups kept up the campaign against Vaughan's conviction and continued to petition Geary for a pardon. In the summer of 1869, Vaughan was pardoned by Geary on the condition that private funds were raised to send her back to England. Elizabeth Cady Stanton and Susan B. Anthony helped raise the money, a death warrant was never signed, and Vaughan returned home.

ENTRY #21

A few months before the arrival of the millennium, everyone's favorite group of hate-mongers, the Ku Klux Klan, decided they wanted to hold a rally in the heart of it all—New York City. Thinking it a wise idea to march in a diverse, multiethnic, Northern city, the KKK went ahead with plans to make their presence felt in Gotham.

Confrontational Mayor Rudolph Giuliani denied the KKK a permit by invoking a rather arcane 1845 state law that prohibited people from congregating in public places in masks. The law was intended to limit demonstrators who might be inclined to commit more crimes with a hidden identity. The Klansmen countered with the argument that they could face personal harm via retaliation if their faces weren't covered up, and thus, denying them a permit was a violation of their right to free speech.

An odd alliance of bedfellows backed the lawsuit filed by the New York Civil Liberties Union on behalf of the Ku Klux Klan. Their right to march was supported by the Rev.

Al Sharpton, and a "friend of the court" brief in favor of the KKK was filed by the *Amsterdam News*, the first such brief filed in the ninety-year history of the influential African-American newspaper. A pair of federal judges sided with the masked Klan, noting that the facial coverings provided protection for those who could face retribution for speaking their beliefs. Mayor Giuliani took the case to a federal appeals court.

Did the Ku Klux Klan have the right to hit the streets of Manhattan? Masked or unmasked?

You be the judge . . .

OUTCOME #21

The federal appeals court reversed the initial ruling and the Ku Klux Klan was allowed to march, but their beloved white masks had to stay at home. Lawyers from New York City attempted to stop the rally, but to no avail, and many free-speech advocates felt Mayor Giuliani's invocation of the 1845 law was a disingenuous ploy to deny the Klan's right to free speech.

As far as the rally itself? About two dozen members of the Ku Klux Klan were greeted by six thousand protesters, some of whom showed their disapproval of hate speech by turning violent against the underwhelming group of Klansmen. But that wasn't enough for those who hate ugly, racist, violent language. There were also attacks against the police detail assigned to offer the KKK protection and the handful of free-speech advocates who still believe in that thing called the First Amendment.

ENTRY #22

A "civil-liability" law was passed in Louisiana that allowed any woman who had an abortion to sue the doctor for up to ten years after the procedure. Not only would the woman be able to sue on her behalf, but also for damages "occasioned by the unborn child." There was no cap on the amount doctors could be legally required to pay if they lost a case, so one woman who regretted her past decision could force the closure of a legal abortion clinic.

A lawsuit was filed by a group of abortion providers who worked at a small clinic. A lower court found the law unconstitutional on the grounds that it would limit women's access to abortions because it would lead to fewer doctors performing the procedure, but the case was heard by an appellate court.

If a woman has an abortion, should she have a decade to sue the doctor? What if she was broke and couldn't care for the child but becomes a fundamentalist Christian five years down the road? Wouldn't all women's constitutional right to an abortion be in jeopardy?

You be the judge . . .

OUTCOME #22

The appellate court threw out the lawsuit filed by the abortion providers, even though it could easily lead to the closure of all clinics through bankruptcy. Many in the abortion-rights movement consider the ruling to be a subversive tactic by the antiabortion movement to deny women their legal right to an abortion. It is an arena that will be revisited by higher courts in the future.

ENTRY #23

Here's a case that we all think we know the answer to because it has been a staple of those who think our litigious society is going to ruin America, and of hack comedians with a severe dearth of material.

It is the infamous McDonald's scalding coffee case. You may think you know what happened, but take a look at the details before making up your mind.

An elderly woman was a passenger in a car that was stopped by the driver for a moment while she added cream and sugar. The woman placed the cup between her knees and tried to remove the plastic lid. In doing so, she spilled the contents in her lap. The sweatpants the woman was wearing absorbed the coffee and she suffered third-degree burns over 6 percent of her body, including her inner thighs, perineum, and genital and groin areas. She was in the hospital for seven days and underwent skin grafting and debridement therapies.

The woman sought a twenty-thousand-dollar settlement

to cover her medical bills, but McDonald's balked, and the case went to court. During discovery, McDonald's produced documents of over seven hundred claims by people burned by its coffee between 1982 and 1992. McDonald's own manual said that it held coffee at between 180 and 190 degrees, which is substantially higher than that maintained by other establishments or of home coffeepots, which normally runs between 135 and 140 degrees. A thermodynamic scholar testified, on behalf of the woman, that liquids at 180 degrees will cause a full-thickness burn to human skin in 2–7 seconds. Further testimony showed that number goes down exponentially, and, at 155 degrees, she would have avoided a serious burn. Although McDonald's said that its customers usually bought coffee on the way home or to work and drank it there, its own research showed that the majority of consumers guzzled their java in the car and that most customers were unaware that they could potentially suffer third-degree burns.

Did the woman have a legitimate lawsuit? If so, how big should the award be?

You be the judge . . .

OUTCOME #23

The jury awarded the woman $200,000 in compensatory damages, which was reduced by $40,000 because the jury felt the accident was twenty percent her fault. The jury also awarded the woman $2.7 million in punitive damages, which is roughly two days of McDonald's coffee sales.

The trial court reduced the punitive award to three times the compensatory damages, $480,000. The final total will never be known by the general public, however, because both parties entered a private settlement.

It has been reported that McDonald's has lowered the temperature of their coffee.

ENTRY #24

Let's revisit McDonald's for another case. This time a man sued the fast-food empire because he sustained injuries in an automobile accident with one of their customers. The man said that the driver who hit him was distracted after spilling a McDonald's chocolate shake while trying to grab a handful of french fries. The lawsuit stated that McDonald's sold the other driver his meal without a written or verbal warning along the lines of "don't eat and drive," which it should have known was the driver's intention.

Did the lawsuit have merit?

You be the judge . . .

OUTCOME #24

This time, McDonald's was not held responsible as the court ruled that the company shouldn't have to warn its customers of the obvious, that eating and driving don't mix. McDonald's wasn't able to recoup the attorney's fees and the case still cost it $10,000 and three years of legal paperwork and minutiae.

ENTRY #25

This is an issue that has been revisited in various ways and in various states in the last few years. Here is one of these cases.

In a town in rural Oregon, mandatory drug-testing was instituted for all elementary and high-school athletes. The tests were administered without any intimation that any individual athletes were using drugs. All boys and girls who took part in interscholastic athletics would be required to submit random urine samples for the mandatory drug screening. The school district instituted the policy to deal with an increase in student drug use and because there was evidence that an athlete had suffered an injury because he used marijuana.

Are the drug tests an unconstitutional violation of the students' individual civil liberties?

You be the judge . . .

OUTCOME #25

A United States Court of Appeals struck down the mandatory drug-screening program because it violated the students' constitutional right to be free of unreasonable searches. The Supreme Court felt otherwise, and ruled in 1995 that random testing of high-school athletes does not violate the Fourth Amendment of the Constitution.

Still, other state courts have issued conflicting rulings on mandatory drug-testing and it is an issue that will surely be revisited again.

ENTRY #26

Here's one to take into consideration before popping the question, because the question might come back to pop you.

A woman filed suit against her former fiancé after the big fella broke off their engagement after a mere seven weeks. She claimed that the pain from the breakup sent her into therapy and kept her from working.

Does the jilted lovebird deserve compensation from her former fiancé? Or, is this breakup even worthy of a court appearance?

You be the judge . . .

OUTCOME #26

Before you buy the ring, consider the outcome of the woman's lawsuit. A jury awarded her $178,000: $93,000 for pain and suffering, $60,000 for loss of income from her job and $25,000 in bills from the shrink. How much would the poor sucker have had to pony up if he had left her at the altar?

Eventually, though, the man experienced nonwedded bliss when the jury's award was thrown out by an appeals court.

ENTRY #27

Sodomy is still illegal in some states and many critics say such laws are used mainly against homosexuals, although most of the laws technically apply equally to heterosexuals (and, food for thought, include oral sex between consenting adults). Sodomy laws are rooted in antiquated religious edicts banning nonreproductive sex that remain on the books even though sexual mores have changed, and thus, the illegal sexual activity is common in the United States. Although the laws are often ignored, gay rights lawyers say that their clients are subject to arbitrary, discriminatory sodomy prosecutions. For example, sodomy laws have been cited as a reason for outlawing gay marriage and adoption.

With that in mind, consider the case of a gay bartender in Georgia, who was charged with having sex with another man in his bedroom. The bartender was never prosecuted, but he filed a challenge against the sodomy statute that made it all the way to the Supreme Court in the mideighties.

Should the Supreme Court have overturned the sodomy ban? What is the key issue in the case for (or against) the bartender?

You be the judge . . .

OUTCOME #27

The Supreme Court ruled 5–4 that the constitutional right to privacy does not include homosexual sodomy. Ironically, the fact that the bartender was never prosecuted or sent to prison may have provided the key swing vote. Justice Lewis F. Powell Jr. wrote that a prison sentence would have created "a serious Eighth Amendment issue" and might have constituted cruel and unusual punishment, although he would later say that he had made a mistake in providing the swing vote. The bartender stayed out of the clink, but the sodomy law stayed on the books.

Eventually, the law was overturned by Georgia's Supreme Court, but a handful of states still have anti-sodomy laws on the books.

ENTRY #28

An HIV-positive California man with the symptoms of AIDS was growing marijuana in his house and backyard because he laced a peanut butter ball with the illegal drug and ate one at every meal to fight off nausea and maintain his weight. Previously, the man had pleaded guilty to growing marijuana, saying he was no longer growing it but would continue using the drug to alleviate his pain.

The man admitted he had little faith in doctors and traditional medicine and said he had watched friends die from AIDS while taking legal drugs to combat the disease. The man felt that marijuana was much better for his health than a drug like AZT. The district attorney argued that since there is no cure for the disease, the man was choosing to use marijuana over other legal drugs, which meant he was choosing to break the law. The man's lawyer asked the jury why her client should have to take the legal medicines and wait for the symptoms to worsen before being allowed to use marijuana.

Was the man's use of an illegal drug to alleviate the symptoms of his pain a medical necessity? Or, was his choice to grow and take marijuana unreasonable, even in light of his mistrust of legal drugs?

You be the judge . . .

OUTCOME #28

Although this kind of case has been ruled upon differently in various courts across the land, the man was acquitted of the two felony counts of growing pot in this particular instance. In a short deliberation, the jury decided that the man had a legitimate medical need for marijuana to combat the HIV virus and try to prolong his life.

ENTRY #29

In Minnesota, the National Labor Relations Board and Equal Employment Opportunity Commission (a federal agency) backed a lawsuit by a group of workers who claimed they were fired by a national hotel chain for starting a union organizing drive. Sounds cut-and-dry, except the wrinkle in this case is that the workers were all *illegal* Mexican immigrants.

Do the workers have a right to organize even if they had no legal right to the jobs in the first place?

You be the judge . . .

OUTCOME #29

The hotel chain didn't have their day in court, because they settled for more than $72,000 with the eight workers, seven of whom avoided deportation and were allowed to remain in the United States by the INS.

ENTRY #30

Here's one for all the fat, lazy, brew-guzzling couch potatoes who feel they've been cheated by their old friend the television. A man sued Anheuser-Busch to the tune of $10,000 for false advertising. His complaint was that the outcome of drinking beer, implicitly implied in their ads, was that women would find him sexy and he would become a liquid Lothario. He filed suit because not only didn't he become a suds stud, but too many beers made him sick.

Did the glamorous girls in the beer ads lead our man to have unrealistic expectations? Did he deserve compensation for gaining nothing more than a hangover?

You be the judge . . .

OUTCOME #30

A Michigan Court of Appeals upheld a lower-court decision and dismissed the case.

Even if his pockets aren't lined, women all across the Great Lakes area should keep their eyes peeled for the staggering, nauseous, lady-killer.

ENTRY #31

A California woman surprised her husband one evening with the news that she wanted a divorce. They couple ended their marriage with the standard legal proceedings, but his ex-wife simply plain forgot to mention to the court that a few days prior she won over a million dollars in the lottery.

A couple of years later, the ex-husband, after filing for bankruptcy, learned the truth when he inadvertently received a letter in the mail offering to turn the lottery winner's money into ready cash. He filed suit against his ex-wife and the case went to court.

Did the ex-husband deserve a portion of his ex-wife's lottery winnings? If so, how much?

You be the judge . . .

OUTCOME #31

The judge ruled that the ex-husband deserved quite a large portion of the lottery windfall, all of it to be exact. The judge penalized the woman for defrauding her ex-husband and the court, which probably became a familiar venue for her because she subsequently filed for bankruptcy.

ENTRY #32

A British woman accused a coworker of raping her at the pharmacy where they were employed. The jury, the majority of whom were women, didn't find her story credible. The woman waited nine months to report the alleged rape, never sought out the assistance of local doctors or police, and store videos from the days following the supposed attack showed her at ease and unbothered alongside her coworker.

The jury felt the man had been through the wringer and held the woman accountable.

Would you penalize the woman who falsely accused the man of rape? And, what would be a sufficient punishment?

You be the judge . . .

OUTCOME #32

The jury ordered the woman to pay $630,000 (£400,000) in damages to her coworker. Some women's groups were up in arms, but the man's barrister in the case seemed to sum up the feelings of the jury when he said that the woman should not be allowed simply to walk away after it was determined that she was a liar.

ENTRY #33

Here's a bit of Irish lore that isn't blarney, but is one of the more amusing legal cases this side of the Emerald Isle.

It seems there was a woman who enjoyed a night out at a local pub, but upon leaving shortly before the witching hour, forgot her coat and briefcase. The woman went back in the pub to retrieve her items and to use the restroom. Apparently the toilet was rather comfortable, because the woman nodded off. She woke up sometime after 2 A.M. to find that everyone had gone home for the evening and she was locked inside the watering hole. The woman spent the night alone in the pub until the staff arrived the next morning.

The woman filed suit against the publican, claiming the establishment was negligent in not checking the restrooms before locking the doors for the night.

Does the pub prisoner have a case?

You be the judge . . .

OUTCOME #33

Though there is many a barfly out there who would consider a night locked in a pub to be a gift straight from the hand of God, the woman's suit earned her an award of four thousand pounds.

A little sidebar to the case . . . one of the initial claim hearings had to be adjourned because the woman's barrister couldn't keep from breaking out in hearty fits of laughter.

ENTRY #34

A Midwestern mechanical contracting firm had a strange initiation that dated back to the founding of the centuries-old company. The boss spanked a newly hired computer analyst twice with a four-foot carpenter's level and announced that "you're one of us."

During the ritual, an employee lifted the man off the ground while another one of the executives sized his behind like a batter in the box and then swung for the fences. The man whose end was the receiving end said that the pain lasted for two days and bruising was evident for over a week. After leaving the firm, he sued for damages.

Goofy? Absolutely. Traditional? In some off-kilter way, sure. But was the initiation worth a large financial reward?

You be the judge . . .

OUTCOME #34

The jury sided with the human piñata to the tune of a cool million, which was later reduced by a county judge to roughly $140,000, the annual salary of one of the top executives. The case went to a court of appeals and they upheld the financial reduction because a million dollars would have severely crippled the company.

ENTRY #35

In Seattle in the early 1990s, a firefighter/Peeping Tom-style auteur set up a video camera in a coed locker room in the firehouse and taped two of his female coworkers changing. The firefighter also made a tape of himself having sex with a woman who wasn't aware that she was being filmed. As if that wasn't enough, the man secretly videotaped the fourteen-year-old daughter of a fellow firefighter as she was wrapped in a towel, coming out of the shower: She heard the camera and alerted her mother when she got to school. In a platonic arrangement, the man was living in the home of a female firefighter and watched her two daughters when she was at work in exchange for rent.

Surely the surreptitiously voyeuristic videotaping broke some law, didn't it? For what crime could the man be charged and found guilty?

You be the judge . . .

OUTCOME #35

If you answered, "the man broke no law whatsoever," you win the grand prize. The only charge prosecutors could come up with was criminal trespassing, but that was a stretch because the locker room was coed and the privacy within was on the honor system. By the time the case was litigated, the statute of limitations had run out on the charge anyway. Furthermore, since the man was living in the home of the fourteen-year-old girl, his behavior wasn't technically trespassing and the content didn't fall within the legal definition of child pornography.

The man was never arrested or charged with any crime, although he was fired from the fire department and a restraining order was issued keeping him away from the house where he had deviously watched over the girls. After a similar case happened in the area, a law was put into effect that made voyeurism a felony if it involved covertly taping, watching or photographing someone without their knowledge for sexual arousal or gratification. Laws, however, can't be retroactively applied, so the man skated and theoretically could have gotten his tapes back.

A postscript in the age of the digital camera and the Internet . . . some states still don't have voyeurism statutes on the books.

ENTRY #36

There are laws on the books in roughly 80 percent of states, but they aren't necessarily enforced in many of them because they haven't been challenged in most state courts.

In Florida a law was passed that made parental or legal guardian notification mandatory at least forty-eight hours prior to an abortion provided to a girl under eighteen. Supporters of the bill believe that parents are the best equipped to help and comfort their daughter, that parents need to be aware of serious medical procedures, that parents need to know about the abortion because of the potential physical and emotional results and that the state requires parental notification for much more frivolous matters, like a minor's obtaining a tattoo.

Opponents of the law believe that, in fact, parents can be the least comforting and that girls should not have to fear potential physical or emotional abuse, that girls may be impregnated by family members, that abortion is such a seriously personal matter at any age that governmental intrusion is an invasion of individual privacy rights, and that notification for trivial matters like tattoos is irrelevant because they are nowhere near as important as the personal, life-changing decision of whether or not to have a baby.

The tough, complex, divisive case went before a circuit judge. Should parental notification be mandatory?

You be the judge . . .

OUTCOME #36

The circuit judge overturned the parental notification law because it violates the girl's right to privacy. He felt that the law, even with its best intentions of preserving families, would too often force the personal decision of a minor toward what the parents want because they could make it difficult for the child if she disagreed with the choice. The case was appealed, and a Florida appellate court upheld the state law requiring that parents or a judge be notified before a minor gets an abortion. The case seems to be headed to the Florida Supreme Court and is sure to recur in different forms throughout the country.

ENTRY #37

In December 1999, six Worcester, Massachusetts firefighters were killed in a burning building. The fire was started at the old, abandoned Worcester Cold Storage and Warehouse Co. by a homeless couple squatting inside when they allegedly knocked over a candle.

The homeless couple didn't report the fire, but the first two firefighters into the building searched for them because they thought the people were trapped inside. After receiving a Mayday call from inside the building four more firefighters went in to find their colleagues who were running out of air. There were no windows inside the warehouse and the four firefighters who went in second got lost in the smoky maze. All six men perished.

Six counts of involuntary manslaughter were filed against the homeless couple and the case went before a judge. The crime of manslaughter requires "wanton and reckless behavior." Was the homeless couple guilty of involuntary manslaughter? Could they be held responsible for the horrific chain of events that left six Worcester firefighters dead?

You be the judge . . .

OUTCOME #37

The judge dismissed the charges against the homeless defendants, who pleaded innocent to starting the fire, because there was no evidence that their actions were "wanton and reckless" despite the tragic results.

ENTRY #38

Let's go back to the origins of the American system of law and order, to the time of the Puritans and the Massachusetts Bay Colony they founded to escape religious persecution in England.

The Puritan officials had a particular beef with the Quakers (AKA the Society of Friends). The Puritans felt that the Quakers wanted to overthrow the tenets of Christianity. So the Puritan colony passed a law that cast out all Quakers under penalty of death. Two Quaker men were imprisoned in Boston, and, when Mary Dyer came to visit them, she was also thrown in the clink. All three were banished and ordered never to return to the colony or face execution. They left for a few weeks, but returned and were arrested, tried, convicted, and sentenced to death for the crime of being Quakers.

The three accepted their fate, but Dyer's husband (who was not a Quaker) was not quite as willing to go along with the execution of his beloved. He wrote a letter protesting the restriction of his wife's religious freedom and noting the hypocrisy of Puritan persecution. Dyer was forced to stand in the gallows with a rope around her neck, but she only watched as the two men were hanged. She was given two days to get out of town for good. Dyer left for seven months, but returned to denounce the Puritan law.

Put yourself in the shoes of the General Court in the Puritan colony, and ask, "What should be done with this rebel, Mary Dyer?"

You be the judge . . .

OUTCOME #38

When she returned, the General Court stood by their law and Mary Dyer was hanged in June, 1660.

The hypocrisy of the Puritan General Court is obvious, but it is interesting to note that there have been incongruities with respect to the rights of various groups in American courts since the first settlers arrived.

As for Mary Dyer, a statue marking her quest for religious freedom stands tall at the State House in Boston.

ENTRY #39

A Michigan man on his first canoeing trip hit a rock, fell in the water, got soaked, and let his feelings about the situation be known in a lengthy profanity-laced rant. The cavalcade of cursing took place in front of a two-year-old and a five-year-old as their parents tried to cover the young'uns' ears. The father said that it wasn't the first time he had heard profanity on the river, but this was an excessive case. The alleged obscenity orator claimed that he didn't know children were present, but the prosecutor argued that he should have seen the family, and the father added that there were lots of kids around at the time of the R-rated tirade.

The man (who had never been in trouble with the law before) was charged under an 1897 Michigan law that barred profanity in public places. An ACLU representative argued that the law was outdated and it infringed on the bawdy fellow's rights of expression. The judge felt that was for an appellate court to decide, although he did rule as unconstitutional the part of the law that made it a crime to swear in front of women. The judge ruled the part of the law that made swearing in front of minors illegal was acceptable.

Should the cussing canoeist be charged under the old law aimed at potty-mouths?

You be the judge . . .

OUTCOME #39

The jury found the foul-mouthed man guilty and sentenced him to four days of community service and fined him $75. It may seem harsh, but he could have been sentenced to ninety days in jail.

There's no truth to the rumor that the jury considered sentencing him to one hour of allowing the children's mother to wash out his mouth with soap.

ENTRY #40

A Georgia police officer's daughter was mauled by a neighborhood German shepherd–husky mix. The dog, Bud, appeared on a chain in the unfenced yard of its owner a week and a half later. The cop took his gun and shot and killed the dog.

Two misdemeanor charges were filed against the cop that could send him to jail for a couple of years and end his career as a police officer. The cop claimed that he was trying to protect the community because Animal Control had done nothing and the dog's owner clearly did not have the animal euthanized. The prosecution said that the police officer didn't follow the proper legal channels and broke the law by taking matters into his own hands at a time when his family was in no imminent danger. The prosecution added that sympathy for the man's daughter did not mask the fact that he broke the law.

Did the canine vigilante go too far? Or, was the police officer being a solid citizen who ensured the safety of his family and the community?

You be the judge . . .

OUTCOME #40

The jury needed less than three hours to acquit the police officer of the charges. The jury foreman expressed concern with the local Animal Control Department and the jury sent a note to the judge asking why the dog's owner hadn't faced any disciplinary action.

The cop's daughter called her father a "hero."

ENTRY #41

A bank discovered that one of its richest accounts was chock-full of embezzled booty. It decided that the prudent course of action would be to return the pilfered money to its rightful owner. After the funds were returned, the alleged accomplice of the embezzler said, "Not so fast—my partner may have been convicted, but I was never convicted of anything." The man filed a lawsuit asking for $20 million in damages.

Is possession nine-tenths of the law? Should the bank be held accountable for transferring the funds?

You be the judge . . .

OUTCOME #41

Cooler heads prevailed and the bank won in court, but still ended up spending twenty thousand mounting its legal defense.

ENTRY #42

A male member of a "sovereign" militia decided that he had reached his limit with the local police after his driver's license was suspended for his having far too many unpaid parking tickets. He did what every red-blooded American would do—wrote up his own liens against the local traffic cops and the judges who heard the cases regarding vehicular infractions. The man forged the names of the "offenders" on his liens and affixed a seal that he designed for authenticity.

The man, however, was by no means unreasonable. He offered to revoke the liens in exchange for the reinstatement of his driver's license. Is this you-scratch-my-back-and-I'll-scratch-yours deal a fair proposition, the kind of wheeling and dealing found in all United States courts? Or, is the man asking for more trouble?

You be the judge . . .

OUTCOME #42

The man was found guilty of various counts of fraud and of attempted criminal syndicalism. The judge took it easy on the enterprising fellow and sentenced him to five years probation . . . which was promptly revoked when it was revealed that the man had neglected to file his tax returns for the previous two years.

ENTRY #43

A tobacco heiress passed away and left behind an estate worth a cool $1.5 billion. She also set up a hundred-thousand-dollar trust fund for her beloved dog, Minni. The executor of the estate thought that the mutt's windfall was rather excessive and went to court to have the trust fund declared invalid. Not surprisingly, the man to whom Minni was bequeathed opposed the motion to declare the trust fund null and void.

Should the prosperous puppy pad its pockets? Or, is the canine's cash grossly gratuitous?

You be the judge . . .

OUTCOME #43

The chew toys and Milk Bones are on me!

The judge denied the motion, and the big bucks have gone to the dogs. The judge ruled that since legal ownership of the dog was separate from legal ownership of the trust fund (it was vested in a separate company), Minni's new owner was the beneficiary and it became his job to ensure the pooch's pleasure free of financial burden.

ENTRY #44

In the early 1970s, a man was convicted of three shotgun murders in the Deep South at the age of 17, but he swore in court filings throughout his time in jail that he was innocent. He was a poor kid from a mobile home community who watched his alcoholic father shoot his mother in the chest, killing her in his arms. One night, he stole a truck and abandoned it near a gas station where an attendant had his head blown off. The next morning he was brought into the local police station and interrogated by a small-town detective (who would eventually be fired for brutality) with a reputation for beating confessions out of suspects.

The boy was grilled for seventy-eight straight hours without a lawyer and was threatened with execution, which wasn't used at the time. Days later, relatives visited him and his body was still covered in bruises. The boy confessed to the killing, as well as another one the same night, and was also charged with the murder of a body that was found in a ditch, even though the death certificate listed no cause of death. The boy said that one of his relatives owned a shotgun, but a relative noted in an affidavit that the barrel was rusty and the gun was covered in cobwebs. The girl he was with the night they went joyriding gave conflicting statements about seeing the killings and then admitted later that she lied. The boy's "accomplice" was also beaten and served ten years for the crimes based solely on a confession that he later said he never read. The boy was convicted on three counts of murder without finding any fingerprints, tire tracks or blood on his clothes, even though the shotgun blasts sprayed blood all over the walls.

The boy legally became a man and decided that he wanted out of the notorious Southern prison he resided in, and a clerk helped him secure a transfer to a calmer prison, from which he promptly escaped and was caught in a bar three days later. A second escape attempt worked when he faked appendicitis by holding in as much water as he could, creating a viral infection in the kidneys. After having his appendix removed, he escaped from the hospital and was found over a week later some three hundred miles away. After years without escaping, the man was granted eight-hour furloughs to visit his new wife (a former pen pal), but the furloughs were rescinded in the "get-tough-on-crime" mideighties. One afternoon, while taking care of a stallion, he hopped on the horse, rode it to the warden's house, stole his car and detoured to see his dying father. He was caught two days later without a struggle and returned to prison.

Twenty-five years later, a lawyer took on his case and the state supreme court ruled that his conviction was coerced and was overturned. The state made no attempts to retry the man, and there is still no evidence linking him to the crimes. The accomplices have since recanted their statements. The man could have walked out of prison a free man, but instead is locked up for life because of the prison escapes.

Should the man, innocent of murder, but guilty of breaking out of the hoosegow, be free to go or face more jail time?

You be the judge . . .

OUTCOME #44

The sad ending to this amazing saga is that the last escape attempt made the crime a violation of the state's "three strikes" policy. Coerced confession or not, the "three strikes" policy mandates a life sentence in prison, which he is still serving today.

ENTRY #45

A couple bought a new Dodge truck from a local dealership, but then sued under Consumer Fraud and Breach of Warranty because the truck couldn't withstand towing the trailers that the couple transported and sold. The couple claimed that the truck made herky-jerky motions and was unsuccessful in towing trailers that fell within the towing and weight limits specified for it. The couple said they had to hire outside towers, and eventually their business was shut down because the truck wouldn't perform, and, ultimately, they lost their house and had to live in a horse trailer.

The dealer said that they offered the couple a new, stronger flatbed truck, but the offer was rejected. The couple claimed the new truck would have cost an additional $5,000, which they didn't have.

Can someone sue because a machine doesn't cut it? Is the couple's troubled truck worthy of compensation? If so, how much?

You be the judge . . .

OUTCOME #45

The jury felt that the couple's automotive nightmares were quite severe. They awarded them roughly $380,000 in compensatory damages, $600,000 in emotional damages and a whopping $83.5 million in punitive damages.

They could probably buy the dealership now.

ENTRY #46

One important case from back in the day, was the Supreme Court hearing of Charles T. Schenck, a general secretary of the Socialist Party in Philadelphia. In 1917, shortly after the United States entered World War I, Congress passed the Espionage Act, which made it a crime to obstruct the war effort. It came on the heels of the Conscription Act, which legalized the draft.

Some fifteen thousand leaflets were printed and distributed, by hand and by mail, urging people to petition for the repeal of the Conscription Act and compared it to involuntary servitude, which is illegal under the Thirteenth Amendment to the United States Constitution. The leaflets came from the Philadelphia office where Schenck was in charge, and he was arrested and charged with sedition for obstructing recruitment and causing insubordination within the armed services. Schenck's lawyers claimed that he was protected by the First Amendment and had the right to voice his opinion on the public issue.

He was found guilty and appealed all the way to the Supreme Court.

Schenck insisted that the leaflets were legal under his right to free speech. The Supreme Court took his argument under consideration and weighed it against whether or not different standards needed to be applied during times of war. Interestingly, the case was based on the publication of the leaflets themselves. There was never any evidence brought that the actual recruitment of any draftees had been obstructed.

Was Schenck guilty of violating the Espionage Act? Or, was he exercising his right to freedom of speech?

You be the judge . . .

OUTCOME #46

The Supreme Court unanimously upheld the lower courts' judgments and Schenck was sent back to federal prison for three concurrent ten-year sentences, one for each count in the indictment. Justice Oliver Wendell Holmes noted in the opinion that the question came down to whether the words "are of such a nature as to create a clear and present danger." He answered in writing, "When a nation is at war many things that might be said in time of peace are such a hindrance to its effort that their utterance will not be endured so long as men fight and that no court could regard them as protected by any constitutional right."

Did things change between World War I and Vietnam? In many ways yes; certainly encouraging young men to avoid the draft wasn't treated in the same manner; but in other ways no, as we will see in out next case . . .

ENTRY #47

In October, 1967, two Roman Catholic priests, Philip and Daniel Berrigan, led a group of anti–Vietnam War activists into the Customs House in Baltimore, Maryland, where some draft records were held. They made their way to the file area, dumped vials of blood into the cabinets, then waited for the police to show up and surrendered without incident. They were charged with, and found guilty of, willfully destroying United States property, mutilating public records, and hindering the efforts of the Selective Service Act.

While awaiting sentencing, the Berrigans led another group of protesters into the Selective Service office in Catonsville, Maryland. They commandeered almost four hundred personnel files and burned them in the parking lot with homemade napalm. They were again arrested and charged with federal crimes, but this time their actions sparked a wave of sympathetic actions and demonstrations.

At their trial, the Berrigans and the other members of the "Catonsville Nine" testified that their moral objection to

America's participation in the Vietnam War led them to break the law. They all recognized that they were breaking the law, but believed that they were saving lives and serving a higher moral cause. Daniel Berrigan made a heartfelt plea to the judge and jury to interpret the law on the basis of human morality and not technical guidelines of what constitutes criminal activity.

The law was admittedly broken, but was the Berrigans' call to the jury to acquit on the basis of a larger human morality a sound argument?

You be the judge . . .

OUTCOME #47

The Berrigans and the rest of the "Catonsville Nine" were found guilty by the jury after less than two hours of deliberation. The case was appealed to the United States Court of Appeals for the Fourth Circuit and the convictions were affirmed. Although the original judge was sympathetic to their beliefs, and the appeals court debated whether the jury should have been able to acquit them in the face of obvious guilt, the case essentially boiled down to the legal tenet that people can't take the law into their own hands. The court of appeals noted, "If these defendants are to be absolved from guilt because of their moral certainty that the war in Vietnam is wrong, would not others who might commit breaches of the law to demonstrate their sincere belief that the country is not prosecuting the war vigorously enough be entitled to acquittal?"

Bottom line, don't mess with the war machine.

ENTRY #48

In the early 1980s, an Alabama father was distressed to learn that his five-year-old son was reciting the Lord's Prayer in his public school class. The state had passed a law that started the day with a one-minute moment of silence in public schools for voluntary prayer or meditation. The father was uncomfortable that the majority of students prayed out loud and those who didn't were made fun of.

He filed a lawsuit in federal court, but Alabama argued that it was simply a moment of silence and kids could choose to pray to any God, or didn't have to pray at all. Lawyers for the father said that religious influence was clear and that the law wasn't being followed as written. The federal district court upheld the law, but it was overturned by the higher court of appeals as a violation of the separation of church and state.

Alabama took the case all the way to the Supreme Court and continued to argue that a moment of silence did not constitute prayer in school. Does starting the school day with some quiet time interfere with the separation of church and state?

You be the judge . . .

OUTCOME #48

Yes it does, ruled the Supreme Court in 1985. Religion was the driving force behind the moment of silence and it was seen as a way around the ban on prayer in public schools. A similar case recently came up over "spontaneous prayer" (which tends to be well organized) at high-school sporting events and it will surely be hashed out in the courts as well. Ask yourself this bonus question: Are "spontaneous prayer" and a "moment of silence" in the same realm? If people are bent on forcing the issue, how could either be stopped?

ENTRY #49

An ex-convict was playing poker in a bar when a man approached him and wanted a hundred bucks. The ex-con refused, so the man whipped out a gun and fired two shots at the man, missing both times. There was a struggle and ultimately the ex-con got the gun, fired the remaining shot into the air and threw the empty gun across the floor.

Unfortunately, it is illegal for an ex-convict to have ammunition and he was charged with possession of a gun by a felon, a federal crime. At his trial, the man argued that it was self-defense, and that he had fired the gun simply to make sure that it couldn't be used against him.

Did firing the gun make the ex-convict a criminal once again?

You be the judge . . .

OUTCOME #49

Yes, but only in the first jury trial because the judge wouldn't allow the man to present a defense of duress. Upon appeal, however, the case was remanded and the jury was allowed to hear the circumstances that led to the firing of the gun. The "well-founded fear of impending death or serious bodily harm" was reason enough for the jury to find him not guilty.

ENTRY #50

Did you know that the human head weighs eight pounds? Did you know that what *was* heard and *wasn't* shown in *Jerry Maguire* ended up in court? That's right, the shoe company Reebok filed a multimillion-dollar breach-of-contract suit against Tri-Star Pictures. Reebok gave Tri-Star a package worth roughly $1.5 million (including freebies) and was supposed to receive prominent product placement in the Cameron Crowe film about a sports agent, Tom Cruise, and an NFL wide receiver, Cuba Gooding Jr.

A fake Reebok commercial that was filmed for the end of the movie was left on the cutting room floor. And Gooding's character wasn't afraid to exclaim "F—— Reebok" when he was angry about stalled contract negotiations, which didn't sit well with the company. Reebok proceeded to take its anger out the old-fashioned way, by filing a lawsuit.

Big Hollywood vs. Big Athletic Company, who's in the right?

You be the judge . . .

OUTCOME #50

We shall never know who completed whom, because the two sides settled the breech-of-contract suit out of court and terms were not disclosed.

Realizing that you probably feel cheated by the outcome, be aware that this case made the book as a social experiment. Please raise your hands if: during the discussion of *Jerry Maguire* squaring off against Reebok, not one person in your circle uttered the phrase "Show me the money!"

That's what I thought.

Let's move on . . .

ENTRY #51

A man in Los Angeles was charged with first-degree burglary for breaking into an occupied dwelling, but his lawyer appealed the first-degree charge. On what grounds? The only legal occupant of the house had died of natural causes shortly before the would-be burglar targeted the house. The lawyer argued that legally the residence was unoccupied.

Does a warm stiff prevent stiffer punishment?

You be the judge . . .

OUTCOME #51

Resting in peace gave the defendant a peaceful respite, and the charges were thrown out by an appellate court.

ENTRY #52

A Dutch couple on vacation in Florida rented a car from Alamo Rent-A-Car and ended up on the wrong side of the tracks in Miami. They stopped at a gas station to ask for directions, and two thugs attempted to rob them. One of the gunmen got frustrated when he couldn't open the passenger door and shot and killed the man's wife. Both men pleaded guilty to second-degree murder.

The attack occurred a couple of years after a string of highly publicized attacks on European tourists in the southern Florida region. A lawsuit was brought against Alamo by the family of the murdered woman, claiming that they failed to alert the Dutch couple that Miami can be dangerous. Alamo responded that the string of attacks was a few years earlier and they had no obligation to warn their customers about the safety of Miami, and that there was nothing on the car indicating that it was a rental.

Should Alamo be held responsible for the murder of a Dutch tourist?

You be the judge...

OUTCOME #52

A jury found for the plaintiff to the tune of $5.2 million.

ENTRY #53

Here's an ugly case from Missouri between a father and his son. The father wanted to rid himself of child support payments, so while his son was in the hospital getting treatment for asthma, he secretly injected his son with blood containing HIV, the virus that causes AIDS. The boy developed full-blown AIDS, and takes strong drugs around-the-clock and is fed via a tube in his stomach. He has come close to death on numerous occasions.

Initially, doctors were perplexed about the cause of the HIV infection and notified the police. The father, a medical worker, became a suspect after he told the mother that she wouldn't receive much child support because their son wasn't going to live long.

The father was found guilty, but of what crime? Is injecting his son with a virus, that could potentially turn life-threatening, attempted murder?

You be the judge . . .

OUTCOME #53

The judge was extremely frustrated, but the toughest sentence he could impose was a life sentence for first-degree assault, which made the father eligible for parole after fifteen years. The judge openly told the man, "You're going to burn in hell" and the state announced that it would press for the death penalty if the boy dies.

ENTRY #54

A California man was down on his luck and he made a bad decision. For $500, he agreed to deliver a package to the Los Angeles FedEx office and send it to Dallas. He knew that the package contained illegal drugs, but he didn't know the type of drug or how much could be found inside. Unfortunately, the package was loaded with nearly seven hundred grams of crack cocaine.

The deliveryman was a manager for a cable television company and was roughly a semester away from his college graduation. He was under financial duress and needed fast cash when he accepted the assignment, but he also knew he was breaking the law.

The man was certainly guilty of bad judgment, but how severe should his sentence be?

You be the judge . . .

OUTCOME #54

This is one of those cases where the type of drug and the amount dictated the punishment under the federal government's mandatory minimum laws. Accordingly, the sentence was mandated by Congressional guidelines and the judge could offer no alternative to the ten-year sentence the man received. The Reagan appointee judge stated his objection to the minimum requirements, noting that in most cases he agreed with them but in this case the defendant got a raw deal. He reportedly said, "One of the basic precepts of criminal justice has been that the punishment fit the crime. This is the principle which, as a matter of law, I must violate in this case."

ENTRY #55

A New Jersey man wanted to become an adult leader of the local Boy Scout troop. As a child he had been an outstanding member of the organization, becoming one of the three percent of Scouts who earned the highest honor, the Eagle Scout badge. As an adult, he wanted to repay the organization. However, soon after becoming an assistant scoutmaster, he was fired and his application to be an adult leader was rejected. The reason, the Boy Scouts told him in writing, was that he was a homosexual, which they felt was contrary to their values. They found it inconsistent with their required Scout oath to be "morally straight." The man's homosexuality came to light after he gave a speech for his college's Lesbian/Gay Alliance.

In response, the man sued under the antidiscrimination statute of New Jersey, which outlaws discrimination in places of "public accommodation" and the state supreme court ruled that the Boy Scouts had illegally fired the man and ordered the organization to reinstate him. The ruling found that the Boy Scouts, which also excludes atheists and agnostics as leaders, was not a private club that can set its own criteria for leadership. The Boy Scouts appealed to the U.S. Supreme Court and argued that the New Jersey high court violated its First Amendment rights.

Did the Boy Scouts have the right to prohibit an openly gay man from becoming an adult scoutmaster?

You be the judge . . .

OUTCOME #55

In a 5–4 decision, the Supreme Court overturned the New Jersey Supreme Court ruling that the man's ousting was illegal under the state's antidiscrimination law. The chief justice said that the state "public accommodations" law violated the Boy Scouts' constitutional right of expressive association. He also stated that the decision wasn't based on views of whether the Scouts' teachings on homosexuality were "right or wrong."

ENTRY #56

A New York man was convicted of buying two pounds of cocaine from an undercover police officer in the mideighties. After a six-week trial, the man was convicted and sentenced to eighteen years to life. The man had a tough time mounting a credible defense because his attorney was catching zzzz's at various points throughout the proceedings. Witnesses, the prosecutor, a juror and the judge himself testified that "Sleepy" caught forty winks at some point every day during the trial.

The defendant moved to vacate the judgment on the ground of ineffective counsel. The Judge, however, went on record as saying that the defendant received a fair trial and effective representation. The man was turned down by the New York Court of Appeals, so he set his sights on the federal judiciary.

Was "Sleepy" fulfilling his duties? Did the man get a fair trial?

You be the judge . . .

OUTCOME #56

After nine years in prison, the man was granted a Writ of habeas corpus, which is a right that gives American citizens a protection against illegal imprisonment. The federal court took into consideration that the man's lawyer was frequently unconscious and granted the habeas relief. After nearly a decade in jail, and lots of nights to sleep on it, the man was released.

ENTRY #57

Is it a crime to do nothing? Here's a case that tested the bounds of that very question.

Two high-school seniors were at a Nevada casino at 4 A.M., when one of the young men followed a seven-year-old girl into a casino restroom as part of a hide-and-seek game he was playing with the girl. The little girl's father was gambling and not paying attention to his daughter, who was raped and murdered by the one of the teenagers. The other young man was with his friend just before the murder and saw him in the bathroom with the little girl. Varied accounts of the tragic events had him either telling his friend not to hurt the girl or being unaware of what was happening. After breaking the girl's neck and leaving her body in the bathroom, the killer confessed to his friend. However, because his friend was worried that they were fifteen minutes late to meet his father, he didn't bother to tell anyone about the murder.

Back home, the friend didn't alert the authorities either,

and the two teenagers even went for a "last supper" at Taco Bell before his buddy was arrested.

The rape and murder was filmed by a surveillance camera, so the guilt of the murderer isn't in question. The issue here is whether or not the friend was guilty of a crime for not potentially preventing the sexual assault or murder after seeing his friend take the girl into the restroom, or reporting his friend's confession to the police afterward. Does the so-called Bad Samaritan deserve prosecution? If so, what would the charge be?

You be the judge . . .

OUTCOME #57

The friend broke no Nevada law, because a private citizen is not required to intervene in a crime that is taking place nor is he or she required to report it. The horrible case led to the passage of a law, named for the little girl, that makes it a misdemeanor (six months in jail and/or $1,500) to fail to report an attack on a child, except where the witness feels that reporting the crime might endanger himself. This law came after the public outcry over the friend's behavior, but take a second look and check if the law really has any teeth. All the friend (or anyone charged under the law) has to do to escape prosecution is say that he thought his life could have been in jeopardy.

In a postscript, the friend couldn't understand why he became an outcast back at school and lamented that he was going to be remembered as a murder witness and not a stellar science student. He went on to a state college, where he was again a pariah, and there were calls to throw him out of school, including a protest from the girl's mother. But since he wasn't guilty of any crime, there was no basis for his removal. The tactful young man also infuriated the general public when he announced that he would "get my money" by selling his story to the tabloid media once the trial started. The murderer pleaded guilty immediately before the trial started, so the friend's big payday will probably never come.

ENTRY #58

A woman called the local police on a domestic violence incident. Her husband kept loaded guns on the property, and she was reportedly afraid for her life. When the cops showed up, they chased the husband and stumbled upon a marijuana farm. They confiscated over six thousand kilograms of pot being grown on property which was jointly owned by man and wife.

Did the woman seal her fate by making the domestic violence call?

You be the judge . . .

OUTCOME #58

Yes, she did. Unfortunately for the woman, she and her husband were sentenced to ten years apiece and forfeited their property to the government. The judge noted that the sentencing didn't seem fair, but he had no ability to act contrary to the federal mandatory minimum statutes.

ENTRY #59

A speeding drunk driver zipped past detour signs and wrecked his car. Later, the driver, apparently angry at the road, sued the engineers who designed it, along with the primary contractor, four subcontractors and the state highway department because they owned both sides of the road.

Is it possible that a redesigned highway filled with detour signs is the cause of a drunk driver's accident?

You be the judge . . .

OUTCOME #59

As a matter a fact, it is. After five years of litigation, the defendants settled the case for $35,000 each. The engineering firm, a small company with fifteen employees, agreed to settle after dropping $200,000 in legal fees trying to get the lawsuit thrown out of court.

ENTRY #60

A Canadian lawyer had a strange dilemma in regard to his client, who was accused of murdering his wife. The court ordered the alleged murderer to undergo routine psychiatric counseling, but the lawyer didn't want his client to be exposed to any treatment before the trial. Why didn't he want the shrinks to poke around in his client's psyche? He was afraid they might cure him and thwart his chances for mounting an effective insanity defense.

Is this the craziest argument you've ever heard? Or, will the psychiatrists hear the craziest argument and ruin a perfectly sound insanity defense?

You be the judge . . .

OUTCOME #60

The court didn't think pretrial treatment would cure a killer and make him sane, so the man underwent psychiatric evaluation.

ENTRY #61

In Montana, there is a law that protects the rights of hunters against animal-rights protesters. One day, a man was charged with violating the hunter harassment law after he stood in front of a hunter who was about to legally shoot a bison outside of Yellowstone National Park. The man argued that the hunter harassment law violated his First Amendment free-speech rights and the statute wasn't fair.

The man was convicted, but it was overturned by a judge who found the hunter harassment law unconstitutional. The Montana Supreme Court then reversed the ruling and a new trial was held.

Is the hunter harassment law in violation of the protester's free speech? Or, are hunters in need of a little legal protection from the animal-rights crowd?

You be the judge . . .

OUTCOME #61

Hunters reign supreme in the great state of Montana. The man was found guilty of breaking the hunter harassment law. He received a provisional 10-day sentence, which was suspended in lieu of performing community service. The state argued that antihunting expressions such as advertisements or door-to-door campaigns were legal ways to spread the message.

There is no word on the bison's whereabouts.

ENTRY #62

A Florida teenager was convicted for cursing at the local police and calling them "crackers." The teenager was in a large group when he was approached by police officers checking if there were any drugs being dealt. He was asked to produce identification even though he had done nothing illegal. His verbal protest was laced with obscenities. He was arrested and charged with disorderly conduct. The police claimed that they feared for their safety but didn't call for backup, and there were no threats from anyone in the crowd.

The teenager was convicted in a bench trial and sentenced to six-months probation, but the case went on to the court of appeals.

Do American citizens have the right to throw four-letter epithets at the police?

You be the judge . . .

OUTCOME #62

A three-judge appellate panel voided the teenager's probation by overturning the conviction, which was based solely on the content of his constitutionally protected speech. The panel ruled that the cops overreacted since there was no interference with police conduct or legal duties, and there were no physical threats of any kind. The defendant's lawyer admitted that slinging curses at the cops isn't the brightest thing to do, but it didn't deserve an arrest.

ENTRY #63

Hished?

How long is long enough to leave a murderer unpun-

A New Jersey woman killed her mother in 1971 at the age of fourteen and was never caught. She confessed to the killing twenty-seven years later, saying she went into her mother's bedroom and shot her in the chest. Originally, she said that she found her mother in the bedroom soaked in blood and heard a car leaving. She claimed she saw a man who looked like her mother's stepfather, but the police couldn't piece together evidence to charge anyone with the crime. A newly created cold-case squad investigated the old murder, and the woman confessed. She was relieved to get the truth out and she said she had been sexually abused by her stepfather and physically abused by her mother as a child.

The woman was a juvenile at the time of the murder, so the question arose as to how she should be charged. In 1971, state law didn't allow a minor to be tried as an adult and she would only have been held until her eighteenth birthday. Initially, a family court judge ruled that she was clearly rehabilitated and there was no reason to prosecute a middle-aged woman as a juvenile.

Should the forty-one-year-old woman stand trial in a juvenile court for a twenty-seven-year-old killing?

You be the judge . . .

OUTCOME #63

The judge ruled that the woman cannot be legally tried as a juvenile. Since the murder took place during the Richard Nixon presidency, all that was possible was a hearing between the prosecution and defense lawyers to determine if she had been rehabilitated. It was more or less a formality.

The state appealed, and the woman explained what happened in exchange for a reduced charge. She admitted guilt, but was treated as a minor and didn't face any jail time.

ENTRY #64

A man in Provo, Utah, owned a few local video rental stores that carried everything from A–Z, with a healthy section of "X" in the back. The business was doing well, until he was charged with selling obscene material. If convicted, he faced possible jail time and would probably have to declare bankruptcy. While awaiting trial, the man's lawyer was racking his brain in the Provo Marriott and hit on an interesting defense.

The lawyer sent an investigator to record all of the sex films available for purchase at the hotel via its pay-per-view channels. He then went and obtained records that detailed the number of locals who watched "adult" entertainment in the luxury of their own homes through cable and satellite providers. Lo and behold, the proudly conservative members of the county were ordering smut flicks at a disproportionately high level. The lawyer, a devout Mormon, argued that the numbers showed that lots of folks in the area were watching porn, so it was common "normal" behavior. A petition supporting the video store owner's prosecution garnered four thousand signatures, which was roughly the same number of local customers who had rented pornography from his store, but twenty thousand videos had been purchased from a satellite distributor in the same time period. The lawyer noted that they were going after a small retailer when the corporate hotel chain in town offered the same style of erotic films.

Did the man with the X-rated videos violate community standards? Or does the community sound like it might have a double standard?

You be the judge . . .

OUTCOME #64

After two trials (the first ended in a hung jury), the man was declared not guilty of all the charges. After the trial, the Provo Marriott ditched the dirty flicks, so, ironically, the man with the video store probably saw a spike in his rentals.

An interesting tidbit: The case, which in just about every other state would never go to trial, was estimated to have cost over $100,000, the most expensive misdemeanor trial in Utah County.

ENTRY #65

A boy standing outside of a national department store chain decided he was thirsty and as luck would have it, there was a soda machine in front of the store. He didn't feel like paying for it, however, so he tried to steal a can. While trying to filch a pop, the machine tipped over onto the boy and killed him. His parents filed a lawsuit against the retailer, claiming that the store was liable for their son's death because steps could have been taken to secure the soda machine and ensure the safety of all children who use it.

Did the parents have a case against the chain?

You be the judge . . .

OUTCOME #65

No, they didn't. The jury found the chain not liable after only two hours of deliberation, partly because witnesses testified about a pattern of destructive behavior by the boy.

Consider this though: There have been a double-digit number of deaths caused by soda machines falling on people in the last ten years. Should vendors be responsible for locking up the large, heavy soda dispensers? Even if it could prevent only one of the more ridiculous ways to die?

Moral of the story . . . use the water fountain.

ENTRY #66

This case sounds like it came straight out of a grotesque horror comic book. A woman actually placed her baby in a microwave, turned it on and killed the infant. She was an epileptic who had gone off medication during her pregnancy and suffered from numerous, extended blackouts.

The woman was charged with first-degree murder, even though she claimed that she couldn't remember the murder ever taking place. The woman's claims of frequent blackouts were verified, so did she deserve to be sent to jail as a convicted killer?

You be the judge . . .

OUTCOME #66

The woman is guilty, in a manner of speaking, because she agreed to a plea of involuntary manslaughter and a five-year jail sentence. What makes this ruling questionable is that it would seem she either killed her baby knowingly and is guilty, or unknowingly and is innocent, and neither qualifies as manslaughter.

ENTRY #67

Deep in the heart of Texas, a sixteen-year-old girl was sexually assaulted and bludgeoned to death, and a man was convicted of aggravated sexual assault and sentenced to ninety-nine years in prison. The conviction was based on confessions he made to three friends after the crime, but the confessions had been disputed. Ten years later, DNA tests found that the man could not have been the source of semen found in the girl's body.

A lower court reviewed the case and said that the man deserved a new trial, but a judge on the court of appeals said that the sentence should stand because the new evidence didn't prove him innocent. She reasoned that the man could have worn a condom, never ejaculated or the victim might have had sexual relations with other men because testimony noted that she was sexually active. The local district attorney, sheriff and a county judge disagreed with the appellate judge and requested that the man be pardoned.

Should the man be freed? At least granted a new trial? You be the judge . . .

ENTRY #67

The governor granted the pardon, and after ten years in the big house, the man was released.

ENTRY #68

A judge was sued by a java salesman who didn't care for the jurist's method of complaining about the rich, robust flavor (or lack thereof) of his coffee. The judge had ordered a court officer to bring the man who ran a coffee cart outside the courthouse into his chambers in handcuffs. The judge then proceeded to loudly berate the man and his coffee for twenty minutes because he hated the taste.

The vendor won an award of $80,000 in compensatory damages and $60,000 in punitive damages. Is this a fair settlement for being shackled during a twenty-minute tirade? Or, was the judge simply expressing his right to free speech in an, albeit, extreme display?

You be the judge . . .

OUTCOME #68

Whether the tar was in the coffee or in the judge's cortex, the trial court felt that he went beyond the role of the robe. The award was upheld and the former judge was removed from the bench for giving false testimony about the incident. Perhaps he is now making cappuccinos at the local Starbucks.

ENTRY #69

A married couple in St. Louis had a novel approach to teaching self-improvement classes. Their sexual improvement "seminars" included show-and-tell. They showed the class their sexual know-how and told them how to implement their "hands-on" improvements to achieve . . . a passing grade?

They only had sexual contact with each other, but they were charged with prostitution, defined as engaging in sexual activity for cash. Their lawyer argued in true Clintonian fashion that they were only demonstrating sexual techniques, which is not sex. He used a golf pro as an example and said that swing lessons don't constitute golfing.

Are these tawdry teachers guilty of the world's oldest crime? Or are the naughty professors simply utilizing their expertise to offer penetrating instructions the best way they know how?

You be the judge...

OUTCOME #69

Class, but not case, is dismissed. A Missouri jury was not hot for teacher and found the couple guilty of prostitution. The jury, however, recommended that jail time wasn't necessary and the couple was fined $300 apiece. They decided to appeal, but in the meantime, they're selling the video from their class (an undercover cop taped it before their arrest) that was shown in court as the "Live Sex Seminar That the Cops Will Watch but Won't Let You See!"

ENTRY #70

A man in Toronto visited friends who had a swimming pool and decided to take a dip. He thought it would be fun to climb through a window onto the roof and jump in, even though the couple warned him that it probably wasn't a great idea. Still, they didn't stop him. Unfortunately, gravity did, and on the fourth jump he broke his neck and became a quadriplegic.

As everyone knows, lawsuits are the *Canadian* Way, so the man sued his friends with the pool. Who is liable for the injuries the man sustained jumping off a roof?

You be the judge . . .

OUTCOME #70

Even the man's lawyer called his actions idiotic, but the jury awarded the rooftop Greg Louganis over two million big ones. The couple was only insured for about a quarter of the amount.

ENTRY #71

Here's a couple of celebrity items (just to make regular folks who have to show up in court know that legal proceedings also nail the rich, famous, and Hollywood Walk-of-Fame types). Bill Cosby was sued for three million clams by a photographer from a New York tabloid who alleged that the legendary comedian assaulted him during a 1992 charity event at the Museum of Modern Art. The photographer said that the "Cos" yanked him out of the auditorium and threw him into the lobby.

Big Bill said that when his wife stood to receive an award from the Coalition of 100 Black Women, the photographer snapped a picture of her without his permission. Cosby admitted he got into an altercation with the photographer, but said there was no assault because he and a security guard simply walked the tabloid shutterbug into the lobby.

Did Bill Cosby overstep the bounds? To the tune of three million dollars? Or, did the paparazzo deserve the heave-ho?

You be the judge . . .

OUTCOME #71

On the one hand, the jury found in favor of the tabloid photographer and ruled that Bill Cosby was liable for the assault. On the other hand, the jury felt that the paparazzo was almost entirely responsible for provoking the "Cos" and so the award was a whopping $2.

A judge later reduced the attempt to the titanic sum of twenty cents.

Hey, hey, hey . . . it's a flaaaaaattttttt settlement . . . and Bill's gonna show you a thing or two . . . about how to win by losing.

ENTRY #72

Outrageous rock/movie star Courtney Love was fronting her band Hole in Florida when two male high-school seniors got right up to the front of the stage, near the mosh pits. Love got angry that the men weren't allowing women to get to the front of the stage, and she jumped into the crowd.

The teenagers alleged that she punched each of them more than once in the chest to get them to back up. Prosecutors added that no artist has the right to come down off the stage and hit a crowd member. Love's lawyer claimed that she waded into a typically raucous crowd, and the boys' claim that she singled them out with punches was solely a way to sue an alternative rock star with plenty of money.

Do the Love taps sound like assault or business as usual in the rough-and-tumble rowdiness of your basic rock-and-roll show?

You be the judge . . .

OUTCOME #72

If a lawsuit is part of your rock-and-roll fantasy, it's time to come up with a new dream. A judge dismissed the charges against Courtney Love because the boys weren't subject to a greater degree of violence than could be reasonably expected at an alternative concert with a band like Hole.

It's only rock-and-roll and she likes it, but Love did state that maybe she would have to reconsider her habit of stage-diving into the arms of all her adoring fans.

ENTRY #73

In Ohio, a case that dealt with the question of whether or not mothers who give birth to children with illegal narcotics in their system have committed child abuse went before the state supreme court. It was ruled that mothers can't be held criminally liable, because the state has different standards for a child and a fetus. The case germinated when a jittery baby was tested and cocaine was found in its blood. The local county department of human services sought and won custody of the newborn. It was the second child born to the mother with drugs in its system, and she would go on to give birth to a third baby with cocaine in the blood.

If the ruling allows for labeling the mother's drug problem as child abuse, it gives family service agencies a stronger case for seeking permanent custody of such babies. The outcome would make it easier for social services to prove the abuse, but is it too easy? This may be an egregious example, but what about a mother who is in drug treatment? Should she have to go through custody battles right off the bat? Isn't that putting an enormous amount of pressure on her? What if the mother's family wants to care for the child? Or, is a woman who uses drugs during pregnancy a clear-cut example of a woman who isn't fit to be a mother? Is the child abuse label merited, making it easier (social workers are usually notified within twenty-four hours) to remove a baby from its mother? Or is the automatic use of the label too rigid?

You be the judge . . .

OUTCOME #73

In a 5–2 decision, the Ohio Supreme Court ruled that mothers who give birth to babies with illegal drugs in their systems have committed child abuse, but did not address the larger, more volatile, issue of whether a fetus is legally a child. The ramifications of the ruling are unclear, however, because most family service agencies already labeled it as child abuse, so even though it is now an official legal definition, what would change? Other states have had different rulings on this issue.

ENTRY #74

Two convenience store owners in Arizona reported that they were robbed at gunpoint (although no weapon was ever found) by a group of gang members. Six-packs of beer worth about $60 were taken. The store was family-owned, and after the robbery two cousins chased the perpetrators down the block and shot at the thieves, killing one. One cousin was charged with second-degree murder and three counts of aggravated assault and his cousin was charged with four counts of aggravated assault for the shooting death. The prosecution alleged that the cousins used excessive force in chasing down the suspects in response to the robbery. The defense argued that the cousins acted in self-defense.

Does self-defense extend past the doors of a convenience store? Or, does it sound like a case of vigilante justice, Quicky-Mart style?

You be the judge . . .

OUTCOME #74

The jury deadlocked and the judge declared a mistrial. In the second trial, a jury acquitted the cousins.

ENTRY #75

A Florida couple found out that at birth their baby had been accidentally switched with another baby in the hospital. The couple found their biological daughter and asked a judge from the Sunshine State to legally declare the girl they didn't raise their biological daughter and give them visitation rights. By this time, the girl was fourteen. The man who raised her had agreed to undergo genetic tests on the condition that the couple would not seek custody of the child. The teenager asked the judge to eliminate the couple's parental rights, in essence, suing to "divorce" her biological parents, so that she could remain with the man she considered her father.

The ultimate question: nature or nurture?

You be the judge . . .

OUTCOME #75

The judge sided with the girl and her father and ruled that the biological parents had no legal rights. And for those of you who love happy endings, the ruling cleared the way for an adoption, making the father/daughter relationship official. Later, the girl returned to her biological parents, but an agreement was eventually reached by all involved that was considered to be in the girl's best interests.

ENTRY #76

A pedestrian in our nation's capital was out living it up when he was hit by a bus. The man, dressed as Batman, was three sheets to the wind as he partied on a public street. The man sued the transportation authority for the injuries he suffered as the crocked caped crusader.

Does the drunken Dark Knight deserve ducats?

You be the judge . . .

OUTCOME #76

Holy windfall, Batman! The man pocketed $600,000 of taxpayer money.

ENTRY #77

A white supremacist in Montana had a novel defense for his crimes. The man had been convicted of a felony in the mid-eighties for selling tainted meat to a school lunch program. He had also run afoul of the law when he drove his speedboat up onto the banks of the Yellowstone River and when he handcuffed a woman to a staircase in his home. He claimed he was holding her for a bail bondsman, but he was fined nonetheless.

In front of the state supreme court, he attempted to have his convictions overturned on the grounds that the jury was not composed of his peers. He argued that the jurors *were not* convicted felons and *were* registered voters, so they couldn't be considered his peers. The man went on to add that the judge hindered his attempts at effective counsel by denying him use of curse words when questioning the jurors.

How exacting does a jury of one's peers have to be? Why can't a white supremacist throw out a few choice expletives? Does the racist deserve to have his convictions overturned?

You be the judge . . .

OUTCOME #77

The Montana Supreme Court upheld the convictions of criminal mischief and disorderly conduct because there was no legal precedent for his arguments to overturn. If you think about it, he was playing with fire because, had his convictions been overturned, then he would no longer be a convicted felon and the next time he finds himself in court his "peers" could feel free to throw the book at him and if he hadn't done any hard jail time . . .

Where's the logic, big guy?

ENTRY #78

A young man in Brooklyn, New York, was seen sprinting away from a building holding his hand to the side of his hip. Now, even though the police officers testified that they did not feel endangered and saw no other evidence of a crime, he was stopped by police and arrested because he was indeed holding a gun. In court, the defense argued that whether or not the accused was, in fact, carrying a loaded 9mm was irrelevant. The case was faulty because carrying one's hand on one's hip is not probable cause for an arrest.

Is a hand on a hip cause enough to "throw the bracelets on a perp" as Det. Andy Sipowicz would say?

You be the judge . . .

OUTCOME #78

Sipowicz might also say, "Quit squeezing shoes and breaking balls and let the young man out of holding." In non–*NYPD Blue* lingo, a judge ruled that there were plenty of other explanations as to why the boy had a hand at his hip and it couldn't be assumed that he was carrying a gun . . . even though he was carrying a gun.

ENTRY #79

One partner in a lesbian couple, who went through a marital ceremony, gave birth to three boys conceived through artificial insemination. The couple eventually broke up and the boys lived with their biological mother, but the other woman continued a relationship with the boys and often provided financial assistance. She operated a successful lesbian bar and eventually moved the boys and their mother into a house she owned.

The boys' mother was stabbed to death, but the case was never solved because the house was badly burned in a fire that was probably set to cover up the crime. Her former partner became a suspect in the murder, so a judge ordered that the boys be placed in the custody of their grandmother. No charges were ever filed, and the killing went unsolved. A custody battle ensued, and it was one of the first cases of a homosexual trying to gain custody of her dead partner's children. The woman told the court that she would sell the bar, open another business, and raise the boys in the suburbs.

Who deserves custody of these kids: the lesbian partner of their mother or their grandmother?

You be the judge . . .

OUTCOME #79

The two parties settled and agreed to be co-guardians of the children. The boys primarily live with their grandmother, but they live with the other woman on alternate weekends, holidays, and summer vacations.

ENTRY #80

Former Louisiana State star Stanley Roberts spent a few years kicking around the National Basketball Association, playing for a handful of teams, until he was ousted from the league for violating its drug policy. Roberts made his way to Europe and was set to sign a $500,000-a-year contract to shoot hoops for a team in Turkey, until the Federation Internationale De Basketball (FIBA) intervened. The federation announced that his ban from the NBA would prohibit him from playing in the FIBA for two years as well. Roberts sued the international federation, claiming that he did not violate the NBA's antidrug policy.

The federation sought a subpoena to obtain Roberts's positive drug test and any grievances he may have filed. The NBA, in turn, didn't want to release the documents because they said that the records were a confidential agreement between the league and the player's association. The NBA was concerned that future collective bargaining negotiations could be affected, because the players' association might not be so willing to agree to an antidrug policy if confidentiality of test results could not be guaranteed.

Lost in the shuffle was the fact that Roberts denied violating the NBA drug program, but should the NBA still be concerned about his future? Should Roberts play for Turkey or is he a turkey who shouldn't be allowed to play at all?

You be the judge . . .

OUTCOME #80

The judge ruled that the National Basketball Association must release the results of Stanley Roberts's drug test to the Federation Internationale De Basketball, which kept Roberts's two-year suspension in effect. The judge noted that the collective bargaining agreement allows the league to issue a short statement saying a hoopster has tested positive for drug use. He added that there was little chance that the information would do serious harm to the interests of the NBA. Certainly nowhere near the damage (followed by the scathing press) that would be done if the players made an issue of the desire to discontinue adherence to the antidrug policy that has been in place for almost two decades.

Somewhere, Steve Howe just took off his high-tops.

ENTRY #81

In 1992, the Canadian Supreme Court heard the appeal of the publisher of *Did Six Million Really Die*? The publisher, Ernst Zundel, had been convicted twice under the "false news" law because his book denies that the Holocaust ever happened. Zundel's book espouses the belief that the Holocaust is a falsehood concocted by a worldwide Jewish conspiracy (and his website portrays him as David fighting the Zionist Goliath). In one of the initial trials, the judge stated that no reasonable person could ever believe that the Nazi atrocities were a myth, which would mean Zundel's beliefs were dishonest. Basically, if the vast majority find his ideas to be nonsense, he must know it is nonsense and is purposely spreading "false news."

The "false news" provision in Canadian law states, "everyone who willfully publishes a statement, tale or news that he knows is false and that causes or is likely to cause injury or mischief to a public interest is guilty of an indictable offense and liable to imprisonment for a term not exceeding two years." Canada, however, basically has the same freedoms of expression as the United States, so messages of hate are perfectly legal. The "false news" laws have been on the books for centuries and seem to have been originally written to keep the masses from rising up against either the King or wealthy landowners.

Ask yourselves this, is there any way to prove that Zundel doesn't honestly believe his ridiculous revisionist theories that six million Jews didn't perish in the Holocaust? Is it constitutional either way?

You be the judge . . .

OUTCOME #81

The Canadian Supreme Court ruled that the "false news" provision of the law violated Mr. Zundel's right to free expression and ruled that the law is unconstitutional. They ruled that a person has the right to knowingly publish false news.

ENTRY #82

Legal Aid lawyers in New York City were preparing and threatening to walk out, and an attorney began wearing a button in court that said, "Ready to Strike." A state supreme court justice in Manhattan ordered the button to be removed on the grounds that it could prejudice clients. A Legal Aid lawyer took her case to an appellate court (surprise, surprise) and said that the button was allowable under her right to free speech. It was pointed out that the supreme court justice had said he would allow non-political buttons that encouraged people to "Save the Whales" or something along those lines.

Would "Ready to Strike" influence courtroom clients, juries and onlookers? Subconsciously? Should the button stay or go?

You be the judge . . .

OUTCOME #82

The button is protected by the Constitution of the United States and other lawyers quickly pinned them to their lapels. The appellate justice noted, however, "If the choice had to be made between saving the lives of lawyers or saving whales, there is little doubt that the overwhelming majority of Americans would come down on the side of the whales."

ENTRY #83

A seemingly happy couple was married for fifteen years when things started to go south, so they sought out a marriage counselor. During an intense session of therapy, the wife revealed that she had never loved her husband. The couple separated and headed to divorce court.

The husband sued his estranged wife for fraud. He said that if she hadn't lied in saying that she loved him, then they wouldn't have gotten hitched and he wouldn't have to give her half of his property and assets in a potential divorce settlement. The wife's lawyers argued that they were married for fifteen years and the husband was just looking for a way around the state's no-fault divorce laws.

What's love got to do with it?

You be the judge . . .

OUTCOME #83

L ove is a battlefield.
  Lack of love is a payday.
The jury awarded the husband over $240,000.

ENTRY #84

A Texan who had been convicted of theft on two previous occasions was arrested after shoplifting roughly $30 worth of meat. Under the Lone Star state's three-strikes statute, the misdemeanor was automatically bumped up to a felony and the man was convicted under the habitual offender umbrella. The judge split the difference on a potential sentence and the meaty thief was sentenced to 50 years in prison.

The man filed an appeal that the sentence violated the Eighth Amendment, which states, "Excessive bail shall not be required, nor excessive fines imposed, nor cruel and unusual punishments inflicted."

Does fifty years in jail equal $30 worth of what . . . ground chuck . . . flank steak . . . rib tips? Did the filcher make his own bed when he knowingly violated the three-strikes statute?

You be the judge . . .

OUTCOME #84

The appellate court upheld the conviction and the fifty-year sentence stood. It's fairly ironic if you consider that the prisoner probably ate $30 worth of taxpayer meals in his first week in jail, let alone the other 2,599 of his sentence.

ENTRY #85

A jury in California heard a four-month trial involving two men who had been charged with keeping a large marijuana garden with the intent to sell the illegal drug. Both men were ill, and they claimed that they had the right to grow it for medicinal reasons, under a 1996 state provision. The legal question of what constitutes acceptable growth for personal use and the wrangling over which Californians can use pot to cure what ails 'em is a long way from being settled. The jury in this trial asked the judge one very important question during the proceedings . . .

Can we wear Halloween costumes?

The jury asked to liven up their civic duty by getting into the spirit of the witching season. Is the jury's request harmless fun or an unnecessary distraction? Is it possible that costumes could tip their hand? Is it fair to ask lawyers to look into the jury box at Dracula, Spider-Man, the Statue of Liberty or Sister Mary Benedict the nun that scared the bejesus out of you as a kid?

You be the judge . . .

OUTCOME #85

The judge laughed and asked the lawyers for both sides what they thought, and nobody seemed to have any rational reason why not, although there wasn't a whole lot of enthusiasm for the idea either. The judge allowed the jurors to play dress-up and didn't put any restrictions on what costumes they could don as they celebrated Halloween in the courthouse. The judge did suggest however that the lawyers come dressed up like the cast of *The Practice*. Whether or not a juror showing up incognito as Jerry Garcia or Eliot Ness revealed too much never had to be addressed.

ENTRY #86

A Texas doctor was in the middle of an ugly divorce and his ex-wife served him with a restraining order—a standard move made in contested divorces that may or may not be based on an actual threat or argument. Whether the doctor deserved it or not is unknown, but afterward he was accused of violating a law that bans anyone under a restraining order from owning a gun. The doctor, unaware of the little-known law, kept his guns and was indicted on federal charges after he allegedly brandished it in front of his wife and daughter. The man was indicted under the Violence Against Women Act of 1994 and a count of illegal firearms possession. His attorney jumped on the constitutionality of taking away his gun under the Violence Against Women Act.

The Second Amendment to the Constitution reads, "A well regulated Militia, being necessary to the security of a free State, the right of the people to keep and bear Arms, shall not be infringed." The debate over how this should be interpreted rages on; gun-control advocates argue that owning a gun is not an individual right, but rather the amendment allows state governments to create armed militias and that handguns and automatic weapons didn't exist when the document was drafted. Gun-owner advocates argue that the amendment is clear and every American citizen has the right to bear arms. The doctor's motion to dismiss the charges was based on the Second Amendment.

The restraining order was given no weight by the judge, who basically ruled that it was a common tactic and there were no extenuating circumstances that made it valid. So, the case came down to this: Does the Second Amendment protect the rights of individual American citizens to own guns?

You be the judge . . .

OUTCOME #86

The Texas judge granted the motion to dismiss on the Second Amendment grounds. He said that the right to bear arms has always been, and should continue to be, an individual right. This case has been appealed to the federal level and may be heard by the Supreme Court in the near future.

Agree or not? Whatever your feelings on gun ownership, the Second Amendment debate won't be abating anytime soon.

ENTRY #87

A man was on a lake with his buddy, who was the step-father of two kids, a four-year-old boy and a seven-year-old girl, who were also enjoying a day on the water. The two men were in the boat fishing and the kids were wearing life jackets while swimming near the boat. The kids drifted too far away from the boat and the two men jumped in to retrieve the kids. The stepfather went after the young boy and his friend went after the girl.

Neither man was wearing a life jacket and the friend started to panic after swallowing mouthfuls of water. He pulled the life jacket off the little girl and she drowned. He claimed that he thought he was going to die and took off her life jacket so that he could hold it on his arm for the both of them. He said the girl accidentally slipped out of hand.

Is it possible the man had the girl's best interests at heart? Should the man be charged with a crime? If so, how severe?

You be the judge . . .

OUTCOME #87

The man was convicted of manslaughter for pulling the life jacket off the girl and watching her drown. The judge sentenced the man to the maximum penalty possible, twenty years in prison, and called it, "one of the most cowardly acts I have ever heard of."

ENTRY #88

A college student was a passenger on a plane that crashed at the Little Rock airport. The fiery wreck killed eleven people on board, including the pilot, but the student was one of the over 130 survivors, although she did suffer a broken vertebra and rib, a concussion, severe lacerations, and multiple cuts and bruises.

The student sued American Airlines for emotional distress. Her lawyer claimed that while she was physically fine and fully recovered from the injuries she suffered, she was traumatized by the crash and is now emotionally disconnected, angry, edgy, won't go into airports, and has become a social misfit. The formerly fun-loving woman is now despondent and is mentally scarred for life, her lawyer said. The lawyer for American acknowledged that the woman was suffering from a form of post-traumatic stress disorder, but added that with the proper treatment she would recover in a relatively short time and be able to pursue her dream to teach music in the inner city.

American Airlines offered the woman $330,000 in compensation; her lawyer asked the jury to ease her pain with a pill of $15 million. Is six-figures enough to cover emotional scarring?

You be the judge . . .

OUTCOME #88

The jury felt $15 million was rather excessive and knocked the award down to $6.5 million.

ENTRY #89

Y ou better not shout, you better not cry, you better not pout, I'm telling you why . . . Santa Claus is coming to court.

A Kentucky woman filed a discrimination suit against her former employer, Wal-Mart, after the company forbade her from portraying Santa Claus one holiday season not so long ago. The woman volunteered to play Kris Kringle, but the experiment failed. One young child accidentally touched Santa's breast and told his mother something along the lines of Old St. Nick actually being Old St. Nicole, and another angry parent complained that she didn't know how to explain a female Santa Claus to her daughter, whose belief in Father Christmas was wavering.

The woman claimed that she had to resign from her regular job at Wal-Mart after the Santa fiasco because her co-workers had a good deal of holiday fun at the expense of her self-esteem. She sued Wal-Mart for over $60,000 in lost wages and pain and suffering. The company claimed that there was no discrimination and that she was dismissed from playing Santa because it was bad for business. Children expected to share their toy-filled longings with a man.

Was the gender-bending Santa Claus the victim of discrimination and deserving of a little gift of her own? Or is the only valid "Santa suit" the red velvet one the big fella wears as he flies through the cold December night?

You be the judge . . .

OUTCOME #89

'Twas the lawsuit before Christmas and all through Wal-Mart, the customer-service reps were happy because their attorneys had done their part.

The fact that the woman got her chance to play St. Nick, ruled out discrimination, said the Kentucky Commission on Human Rights but quick.

It's too bad the woman didn't make a worthy Santa Claus, but if it's not good for business it doesn't help Wal-Mart's cause.

The customers heard the retailer exclaim as they picked up cheap buys, Merry Christmas to all, *and all our Santas are guys!*

ENTRY #90

S ometimes you want to go where everybody knows your name, and they're always glad you're a metallic cyborg capable of spitting out one-liners and giving the animatronic impression of guzzling mugs of domestic beer.

George Wendt and John Ratzenberger, better known as the barfly buddies "Norm" and "Cliff" on the television classic *Cheers* filed suit against the corporate proprietor of a chain of airport bars bearing the same name as the show. The bars featured robot characters, one fat and the other dressed as a mailman, that recalled the famous characters. Wendt and Ratzenberger sued the chain, even though the bar owner properly licensed the copyrights to the characters from Paramount, the studio that owned them. The two men asserted their "right-of-publicity," established under a California law that allows a plaintiff to seek damages if their voice, likeness, name, photograph, etc. is used for an advertisement or sale of a product of which they don't approve.

The initial case came down to the issue of whether Wendt and Ratzenberger had a "right of publicity," because Paramount owned the copyrights to the characters. Should Norm and Cliff be allowed to proceed with their suit against the chain? Or, since the beloved boozehounds are Paramount's property, should they even have a say?

You be the judge . . .

OUTCOME #90

Making your way in the cyberworld today takes every-thing you got, especially when the lawsuit can go forward against the brew-swilling robot.

Basically, it came down to an issue of privacy, not profit. The court ruled that the "right of publicity" trumps the federal copyright, but they aren't at odds with one another, so Wendt and Ratzenberger can sue the chain.

At last call, the two television suds-soakers settled with the chain in a confidential agreement.

ENTRY #91

A couple divorced after an eight-year marriage, but they couldn't determine in what religion their five- and seven-year-old daughters should be raised. They asked a judge to decide how the girls should be raised. The mother converted from Catholicism to Judaism before the wedding and returned to the Roman Catholic church after the divorce. She felt their daughters should be raised ecumenically, but her husband wanted their children to be raised as Jews, because up to that point they had been raised in the Jewish faith.

Church, synagogue or both?

You be the judge . . .

OUTCOME #91

Mazel Tov! The judge declared the children Jewish and granted the father "spiritual custody." He ordered the mother to raise them as such, forbade the promoting of other religions, and sentenced her to 10 days in jail for contempt of court after she took the kids to Catholic services.

ENTRY #92

There are frequent examples of little-guy plaintiffs receiving settlements from deep-pocketed corporations, but does it ever work the other way? Here's a case that pitted a corporate David against a minimum-wage Goliath.

After a female African-American Taco Bell customer in Oconomowoc, Wisconsin, made widely publicized claims that an employee serving her food, used a racial epithet and said, "I just spit in that . . . food," the allegations and publicity led to a sharp drop in business. Taco Bell Corp. filed a counterclaim that the woman defamed the corporation. There were numerous inconsistencies in the woman's testimony, and her past plea of guilty to fraudulent use of a credit card was revealed.

The jury didn't buy her story of discrimination, but were her allegations enough to defame the fast-food giant?

You be the judge . . .

OUTCOME #92

The jury found that the woman did defame the Taco Bell Corp. when she accused one of their employees of racial discrimination. They awarded Taco Bell, the original defendant in the case, $1,060—roughly a buck a day since the alleged incident, which, coincidentally would purchase over five hundred gorditas.

ENTRY #93

A white St. Louis schoolteacher encouraged her eleventh-grade class of African-Americans to write dramas from their personal experiences. Many of the students wrote about sex, pregnancy, drug use, gang violence, and dysfunction in the home. The students acted out the dramas, which contained street lingo and the use of 150 expletives, including "nigger" and "bitch."

Months later, the principal heard a tape of the dramas and called the teacher into a meeting with district officials. She was instantly suspended for allowing profanity in the classroom and was fired after five days of hearings. The teacher felt that she was being discriminated against by the African-American officials who objected to black students using profanity. She took her dismissal (and its repercussions) to the courts.

Did the teacher deserve her job back?

You be the judge . . .

OUTCOME #93

In the initial trial, a jury found that the teacher's First Amendment rights had been violated and that she had been the victim of discrimination. They found no legitimate academic interest in prohibiting profanity in her creative writing class. She was awarded $250,000, and the judge ordered her reinstatement with full back pay and lost benefits, the removal of any reference to her termination, and that the school district pay her attorney fees.

The school district appealed and a U.S. Circuit Court of Appeals reversed the jury's decision. They found that the district had the right to require teachers to adhere to a policy banning profanity and that there was no discrimination. The Supreme Court upheld the decision when it refused to hear the teacher's appeal in the spring of 1999.

ENTRY #94

Here's an oddity from the Great White North. It seems there were five men on trial for two execution-style murders. After a six-month trial, the jury found them not guilty and they were free to go. One woman on the jury was thrilled with the verdict because she had been sleeping with one of the accused murderers throughout the trial.

When this was discovered, she was charged with obstruction of justice. Her lawyers argued that the judge never explicitly instructed the jurors not to have any contact with the accused. The woman also took her case to the court of public opinion, and posted a personal website detailing the witch-hunt to which she had been subjected. She said "I have been tried and convicted for my 'immoral' choice of lover, my short skirts, and my outspokenness."

Getting off with a defendant who is trying to get off might be awkward, but should the juror go to jail?

You be the judge . . .

OUTCOME #94

The juror can only hope her tryst with the accused was enough to tide her over for eighteen months, because that was how long she was sentenced to jail for obstruction of justice. Do you get the feeling the producers of *Ally McBeal* are chomping at the bit on this one?

ENTRY #95

Three children in Milwaukee, ages sixteen, fourteen, and seven, had a request for the family court judge who granted their parents' divorce. They wrote the judge and asked that ties to their abusive father be disjoined, in effect they wanted a divorce from Dad. They wanted his rights as a father rescinded because the constant abuse, primarily mental, had taken a severe toll on their mother's health and well-being.

The judge assigned an attorney to look into the children's claims of physical and mental abuse. The attorney found that the father had taken his kids to the bar with him, used drugs with the oldest one and repeatedly threatened to kill his ex-wife and offspring. The father had been in and out of jail on various fraud charges and told the judge that he had been through alcohol treatment programs and would try to stay on the straight and narrow, anything to keep in contact with his kids. He denied that he ever physically abused them, praised his ex-wife for trying to keep the family intact and said he wanted what was best for the children.

The termination of parental rights happens on occasion, but it is normally a clean break, physically and financially. The attorney for the children wanted the father to lose all visitation rights, but to continue child support and keep the children's inheritance rights.

If a father is permanently cut out of the lives of his children, should he still have to support them?

You be the judge . . .

OUTCOME #95

The judge severed all ties between the father and the teenagers and suspended his relationship with the youngest child indefinitely. The decision ceases all visitation rights, but the judge ruled that the father is on the hook for child support until the children turn eighteen.

ENTRY #96

Here's a unique defense that might make you rethink those first-class tickets to Hawaii . . .

A Northwest Airlines pilot and his crew on a Midwest route were seen at a bar, even though they were scheduled to fly at six-thirty the following morning. An anonymous tip came in that they were violating the FAA's "bottle-to-throttle" regulation that prohibits drinking within eight hours of takeoff. An FAA inspector met them at the flight, and was concerned about their alcoholic breath, bloodshot eyes and the large gash on the pilot's forehead. The inspector was unaware, however, that he could ground the flight and the pilot and crew took off and landed without incident.

They were met by more inspectors who took a blood alcohol reading from the pilot of almost .13, well above the FAA limit of .04, and higher than the state's former drunk driving standard of .10. Initially, the crew said they had a couple of drinks and left at eight-thirty, but an investigation revealed that the pilot was there until after eleven, consumed over fifteen rum-and-Cokes and sliced open his forehead when he fell off the table.

The pilot entered rehab right away. At the trial, his legal counsel came up with a two-pronged defense and said the defendant landed the plane safely and that the booze didn't cloud his judgment and abilities because he's an alcoholic. The logic was basically as follows: Since the pilot was an alcoholic, he had flown planes in that condition before, which was proven by the flawless takeoff and landing.

Does the pickled pilot's defense fly?

You be the judge . . .

OUTCOME #96

I n a manner of speaking . . . sort of. The judge was not im-
pressed with boozy flyboy's defense and sentenced him
to more than a year in prison. So exactly how did the rum-
soaked aviator come out with his wings intact? The Americans with Disabilities Act (ADA) protects alcoholics who
enter a rehab program. Instead of running the risk of going
afoul of the ADA, Northwest rehired the pilot after he got
out of jail, and he went back to flying passenger jets, eventually earning back his captain's stripes.

President Clinton pardoned the pilot in January 2001,
but you may still want to keep a watchful eye on those mini-
bottles . . .

ENTRY #97

A woman in Alaska came up with an interesting plot to score some cash in a hurry. She told everyone in her office that she was pregnant with twins. She received more than $500 in money and gifts, and a few months later told a coworker that the twins had been delivered stillborn in the back of an ambulance. A memorial service was donated by a local funeral home at a cost of roughly $850. The coworker told the suspicious story to a police officer, who investigated the bogus tale, which quickly unraveled and the women appeared in court.

She had been previously convicted of stealing over $10,000 from a bank where she had been a teller. The total amount of the pregnancy scam made it felony theft. The woman told the judge that it wasn't a scam, and she thought she was pregnant. Her lawyer added that the woman had miscarried before, and her husband pressured her to have a baby with hints that he would leave her if she didn't. The judge noted that, either way, at some point she knew she wasn't pregnant and didn't tell anyone.

Does faking a pregnancy and making a buck or two off of it constitute a crime?

You be the judge . . .

OUTCOME #97

As a matter of fact, it does. The woman was sentenced to 360 days in the clink, with all but five suspended, ordered to undergo mental health counseling, repay the funeral home, and let future employers know of her criminal record.

ENTRY #98

A five-year-old boy tragically drowned in the town of Hallandale, Florida, and the boy's mother and grandmother felt the city was negligent in his death. The boy drowned while taking swimming lessons as part of a summer camp in Hallandale and the mother alleged that there was inadequate supervision and that the personnel hadn't properly inquired about her son's swimming abilities. The city of Hallandale countered that the boy's grandmother had signed a waiver relieving the city of legal liability if a camper is injured or dies at the camp.

Both mother and grandmother had the official capacity to sign documents on the boy's behalf, but the grandmother never showed the notarized document granting them both legal authority to the summer camp. The mother filled out the summer camp papers but never signed the waiver. The papers got lost, so the grandmother filled them out instead, and she did sign the waiver without telling the boy's mother.

When the boy started camp, though, he had not been signed up for swimming lessons and didn't know how to swim. Neither mother nor grandmother remembered seeing a camp brochure, which asked the children to bring a towel and a bathing suit every day, so they didn't know swimming was part of the daily activities. The boy's grandmother packed him a towel and a change of clothes, but said that she always put the items in his backpack.

The boy told counselors that he wanted to go swimming and that he had received permission from his grandmother. The boy got away from the group and drowned in the shallow end of the pool, even though there were two lifeguards on duty and a counselor watching the kids. He died the next day and his mother filed suit.

Does the liability waiver, which the grandmother mistakenly signed, protect the city of Hallandale from any legal responsibility in the drowning death? Or, is the city negligent because they didn't test the boy's swimming capabilities, pay close enough attention at the pool or make sure to let the boy's mother know that swimming was a major summer camp activity?

You be the judge . . .

OUTCOME #98

A jury awarded the family $17.5 million. They offered to settle with the City of Hallandale for $7 million, but the town officials planned on appealing the decision. Ultimately, the city commissioners agreed to pay $1.9 million to the mother.

ENTRY #99

Someone brought a dog to the circus in the midfifties and let the pooch run around without a leash. The pooch yapped at an elephant and scared the giant circus attraction half to death. The circus elephant, Buffa, went wild and knocked over a stall, which fell and injured a midget.

The midget sued the circus, and the elephant's handler argued that Buffa did not have a ferocious temperament and thus shouldn't fall under any rigid definition regarding injury from a wild animal.

Is Buffa to blame?

You be the judge . . .

OUTCOME #99

We can't say for sure if Buffa was at fault, but the midget was no Dumbo, because the court held that as a general matter of law all elephants are dangerous animals. The amount of his award is unknown, but this bit of wisdom from the court is priceless. "If a person wakes up in the middle of the night and finds an escaped tiger on top of his bed and suffers a heart attack, it would be nothing to the point that the intentions of the tiger were quite amiable."

ENTRY #100

A woman sued her former employers because they dismissed her after refusing to deal with her major problem . . . sharing an office with an excessively flatulent coworker.

The woman, who had worked at the accounting firm for eight years, was given a new officemate in the middle of June. She quickly ascertained that the male colleague was constantly fouling the air. She wasn't the only one who noticed and claimed the rest of the staff was painfully aware as well. In September, after walking into an odorous funk, she made her first complaint to one of the bosses who jokingly inquired if the fellow had had one too many beers the previous evening. The boss promised the woman he would take care of the situation, but nothing had taken place by the first week of October when the woman became physically ill. The woman was five months pregnant at the time and said that being in close quarters with her gassy coworker made her sick on numerous occasions.

Apparently her coworker began training for a sporting event, so he changed his dietary habits throughout the fall and the problem subsided. Unfortunately, winter set in and the man needed a fire in his belly and the problem returned like the annual Christmas ham. The woman was forced to keep the window wide-open during the cold because she couldn't handle the stench. Finally, in mid-January, she reached her breaking point and told the boss that she refused to work in that office any longer. The boss said he never could figure out how to broach the subject with her colleague, but she was more than welcome to quit.

In court, the boss said that the woman never wrote down her complaints and she gave him all of five minutes' notice. She left during the height of the accounting season because she didn't want to do all the work, which left him in a bind.

Does the woman's case stink?

You be the judge . . .

OUTCOME #100

In the end, we all smell a little bit, but this case reeks of nothing but an amicable resolution as both parties agreed to an out-of-court settlement.

AFTERWORD

In the words of Otto von Bismarck, "If you like laws and sausages, you should never watch either being made."